THROUGH THE BLOOD AND THROUGH THE FLOOD

Putting Your Past Behind You

Kirk A. DuBois

First Printing 2007
ISBN #978-0-9673727-5-4

Printed in USA

CONTENTS

chapter 1

Deliverance Through the New Birth

Knowing this, that our old man is crucified with him, that the body of sin might be destroyed, that henceforth we should not serve sin. For he that is dead is freed from sin. Now if we be dead with Christ, we believe that we shall also LIVE *with him.*

—Romans 6:6–8

In these verses of Scripture written by the Apostle Paul, we see two of the most important truths in the Bible.

First, if you have become a born-again child of God, you are dead to sin.

Second and most important, as a child of God you are also alive in Christ! That is, you have died to your past sinful life and have been "born again" into a new life. In other words, you are a dead man who has been made alive.

On March 9, 1971, I knelt down and prayed, asking Jesus Christ to come into my heart and become my Lord. I was born again. I was only 16 years old then, but I had already lived a whole lifetime. I had been raised in a home filled with strife, fighting, and the ever-present threat of divorce. My dad was gone from home six to nine months at a time while overseas in the U.S. Navy. My mother worked and went to school late into the evenings as a nurse. My older sister helped raise my brother and me.

I had my first negative encounter with the law at only four years old. I was a willing accomplice to some neighborhood youths in vandalizing a house. In my mind I can still see the police officer standing over my bed and talking to me after I had been punished by my father.

By the time I hit the teenage years I was already experimenting with drugs, smoking, and drinking. Before I gave my life to the Lord at 16 years of age, I had been suspended from school for using drugs and explosives, and I had finally been expelled for breaking into several schools. I had run away from home and been caught. I had become a "ward of the State of California," which meant that if I got into trouble with the law one more time, I would be put in a foster home.

On top of all this, I was involved in the occult. I had been searching for God and the meaning of life. That search led me to take part in séances, experiments with extra-sensory perception, meditation, hypnosis, and even witchcraft.

In the midst of all this I heard about the "Jesus Movement" that was taking place among the young people and hippies. Kids just like me who had tried everything were finding what they had been searching for in Jesus. One night I asked God to have someone from that group talk to me if that was what I needed.

The next day while I was in the midst of buying drugs, someone witnessed to me about Jesus Christ. He prayed for me and a peace came over me from head to toe. I was unable to get high on drugs that day, no matter how many I took. It was evident to me that something was happening inside me.

Two weeks later I learned about a group of these "Jesus People" in San Diego where I was living. I made my way to their house, and that is where, as a 16-year-old, I bowed my knees and gave my life to Jesus Christ.

When I stood up I was a new person. The old Kirk was gone forever! I was a brand-new creation. The very next day at school I was right back in the middle of my drug-using friends. This time, though, I wasn't indulging in the free flow of drugs being passed around. Instead, I was telling them how Jesus had changed my life. From that day until now I have been a child of God.

I had both died and been born in one day! I died to the world and I was born into the Kingdom of God.

The day I was born again, in the obituaries of hell, it read:

"Died this day of supernatural causes: Kirk DuBois. Survived by his former father, the devil, and his former family, the world."

The birth announcements in Heaven read:

"Born this day into the family of God: Kirk DuBois, to his proud Father, the Creator—God."

Prior to our New Birth, we had a corrupt, sinful nature.

Ephesians 2:2–3

2 Wherein in time past ye walked according to the course of this world, according to the prince of the power of the air, the spirit that now worketh in the CHILDREN OF DISOBEDIENCE:

3 Among whom also we all had our conversation in times past in the lusts of our flesh, fulfilling the desires of the flesh and of the mind; and were BY NATURE THE CHILDREN OF WRATH, even as others.

We were part of the devil's family, the world system. We were destined for the wrath of God. Thank God for the next two words in verse 4!

Ephesians 2:4–5
4 BUT GOD, who is rich in mercy, for his great love wherewith he loved us,
5 Even when we were dead in sins, hath quickened us together with Christ, (by grace ye are saved).

Because of the death, burial, and resurrection of Christ, we have been delivered from our old nature and have been born again with the nature of God.

2 Corinthians 5:17
17 Therefore if any man be in Christ, he is a new creature: OLD THINGS ARE PASSED AWAY; behold, all things are become new.

"Old things" means your old life of sin and bondage, guilt, shame, harmful habits, failures, and so forth. It has "passed away." It is dead! And everything we need to live victoriously in this life—right now—Jesus purchased for us at the Cross of Calvary.

In John chapter 8, Jesus told a group of people who had believed in Him, *"If ye continue in my word, then are ye my disciples indeed; and ye shall know the truth, and the truth shall MAKE YOU FREE"* (John 8:31–32).

Many Christians today act as if they were short-changed when they received their salvation. From their behavior, you would think that Jesus made an exception in their case and they were not made free. They have not continued in His Word long enough to find out the truth about their "new self" in the Lord. They are still looking elsewhere for answers to their problems. It seems that no one has told them what Bible salvation is really all about!

But what good is a "God" or "Jesus" who can't meet all your needs? Do you mean to tell me that the Creator of the universe—the One Who raises the dead, Who lifts up one nation and brings down another, and Who will one day roll back the heavens like a scroll, consume this present world, and create a new one—cannot handle your problems?

Do you mean to tell me that this God cannot handle your mental and emotional struggles? Or that He can't deal with your sense of guilt or inferiority? Or that He can't heal a part of your body that isn't working right? Or that He can't supply all of your financial and material needs in this earth?

When people really see what God did to them, in them, and for them through Jesus in salvation, they will stop looking to cheap, imitation methods to help them, and they will begin to taste of the sweet victory purchased for them at Calvary!

This book doesn't offer any cheap imitations; it offers the truth as found in the Word of God—the Bible. And if you grab hold of the truth, you will be made free—not because of some eloquent words I may write, but because of the power of the Word of God!

I will show you in the next few pages how we can be delivered from and live a life free of the past and all the lies of the enemy.

Let the truths I share from my heart help you snap the chains of bondage you may be living in now and begin to walk in the freedom Christ purchased for you at Calvary. My fervent prayer is that when you put this book down, you will rise up shouting the famous words, "Free at last! Free at last! Thank God Almighty, I'm free at last!"

chapter 2

A New Marriage

Know ye not, brethren, (for I speak to them that know the law,) how that the law hath dominion over a man as long as he liveth? For the woman which hath an husband is bound by the law to her husband so long as he liveth; but if the husband be dead, she is loosed from the law of her husband. So then if, while her husband liveth, she be married to another man, she shall be called an adulteress: but if her husband be dead, she is free from that law; so that she is no adulteress, though she be married to another man. Wherefore, my brethren, ye also are become dead to the law by the body of Christ; that ye should be married to another, even to him who is raised from the dead, that we should bring forth fruit unto God.

—Romans 7:1–4

The Apostle Paul said a married couple was bound to their marriage as long as both partners were still living. It was only after one spouse died that the other person was free to marry again.

No matter what one or the other partner would do to break that marriage relationship, they were still bound to each other until one of them died.

Now it is not my intent, nor is it the purpose of this book, to discuss marriage and divorce with all their implications and different doctrinal points of view. I am simply doing what Paul did—using a biblical principle to show you a *far greater application of truth.*

1. We were once married to the law of sin and death.
2. We were bound to that relationship as long as we were not born again.
3. It was impossible for us to get free from that relationship in our own ability or by our own actions.
4. Our "old self" died with Jesus Christ on the Cross.
5. When Christ rose from the dead, we rose with Him. We were released from our first marriage to the law of sin and death and made free to be married, or joined, to another—Jesus Christ.

Galatians 2:19–21
19 For I through the law am dead to the law, that I might live unto God.
20 I am crucified with Christ: nevertheless I live; yet not I, but Christ liveth in me: and the life which I now live in the flesh I live by the faith of the Son of God, who loved me, and gave himself for me.
21 I do not frustrate the grace of God: for if righteousness come by the law, then Christ is dead in vain.

Death means separation. We were separated from the law of sin and death when Christ died on the Cross in our place! When He died, we died.

Jesus said, *"Verily, verily, I say unto you, Except a corn of wheat fall into the ground and die, it abideth alone: but if it die, it bringeth forth much fruit"* (John 12:24).

In this verse of Scripture, Jesus was speaking of Himself just before He went to the Cross. He was saying that a seed must die before it can bring forth fruit and that through His death, He would bring forth much fruit.

When a kernel of corn is planted in the ground and dies, it contains within it all the genetic code needed to produce hundreds more just like itself. This happens through a kind of resurrection. You see, when life-giving water hits that dead kernel in the ground, life begins again in it. This time, though, it takes on a new form. It breaks through the ground and grows into a corn stalk, producing hundreds of corn kernels. It has reproduced itself.

When I was a young boy, I liked to grow plants from seeds in science experiments. I used to plant seeds in a glass jar with cotton in it so I could watch them sprout. Once in a while, I would open up a seed instead of planting it. For instance, I would split a bean seed in half. There inside the seed, I would see the tiny beginning of a bean plant. The future full-grown plant was right there inside that seed!

Now if we could look inside the heart of Jesus Christ before His crucifixion, we would see you and me and the rest of mankind. The Church, made up of believers in Jesus, is the "harvest" of the seed Jesus planted—His own life sacrificed for all.

We who believe in Him are the "much fruit" Jesus talked about in John 12:24! In that verse, Jesus was speaking not only of Himself coming forth from the grave, but also of the salvation of all mankind. And that includes you! He was speaking of your death, burial, and resurrection with Him!

We call this the "vicarious" death. This means that Jesus died in our place, as our substitute. He took on the sins of the whole world when He died on the Cross and went into that grave. Then when He rose again, the entire human race, including you and me, rose with Him!

Two thousand years ago angels rolled back the stone from the mouth of the tomb where Jesus' body had lain for three days. When that happened, He burst forth from the grave, and you and I burst forth with Him! He rose like a sprouting seed shooting up through the soil, and we were born again in Him. Through His resurrection, Jesus made it possible for all who would believe in Him to experience the New Birth.

Romans 4:24–25
24 But for us also, to whom it shall be imputed, if we believe on him that raised up Jesus our Lord from the dead;
25 Who was delivered for our offences, and was raised again for our justification.

Colossians 2:12
12 Buried with him in baptism, wherein also ye are risen with him through the faith of the operation of God, who hath raised him from the dead.

When you become a Christian, the same power that enabled Jesus to rise from the dead resides within you.

Romans 8:11
11 But if the Spirit of him that raised up Jesus from the dead dwell in you, he that raised up Christ from the dead shall also quicken your mortal bodies by his Spirit that dwelleth in you.

Jesus purchased salvation for everyone. He freed us once and for all from having to pay the price for our sins. Through

His death, burial, and resurrection, Jesus made salvation available for all mankind—including you if you will accept it.

Grab hold of this marvelous truth: everything mankind lost through the sin of Adam has been restored to mankind through Jesus Christ. Because of Jesus, we have had the following restored to us:

- Right standing with God
- Communication with God
- Innocence before God
- Dominion over the devil

We have a new position. Because we died with Jesus, we are free *from* our former marriage to the law of sin, and we are free *to* be married, or joined, to Christ (spiritually speaking). When we accepted Jesus Christ as our personal Savior, we became legally free from our old marriage to Satan and were made legally free to enter into our new marriage to our Lord and Savior.

We are now in a marriage covenant with Christ!

Romans 7:4
4 Wherefore, my brethren, ye also are become dead to the law by the body of Christ; that ye should be married to another, even to him who is raised from the dead, that we should bring forth fruit unto God.

Ephesians 5:30–32
30 For we are members of his body, of his flesh, and of his bones.
31 For this cause shall a man leave his father and mother, and shall be joined unto his wife, and they two shall be one flesh.
32 This is a great mystery: but I speak concerning Christ and the church.

The marriage covenant is one of the strongest unions that can be made. Believers in Jesus Christ are united with Him in such a covenant.

1 Corinthians 6:17
17 But he that is joined unto the Lord is one spirit.

chapter 3

Through the Blood

And the blood shall be to you for a token upon the houses where ye are: and when I see the blood, I will pass over you, and the plague shall not be upon you to destroy you, when I smite the land of Egypt.

—Exodus 12:13

When the Israelites left Egypt, they left through the blood and through the flood. This is a type or example of what we experience through the New Birth. In this chapter we will discuss the blood. The Israelites came out of bondage in Egypt after the blood of a sacrificed lamb had been applied to the top and side posts of the doors of their houses. The application of the blood was the final and most significant part of the process of their deliverance.

You are probably familiar with the story. The nation of Israel, which had once been prosperous in the land of Egypt, had been reduced to slavery by the time of their exodus. The Egyptians oppressed them and persecuted them severely. They cried out to God, and He heard their cry and raised up a deliverer for them named Moses. This man would lead the Israelites out of bondage and into the land God had promised to their forefather Abraham.

But Pharaoh would not let the Israelites go free without a fight! (This was a bad decision on his part!) So God sent 10 plagues against Pharaoh and the land of Egypt. Each plague was a direct judgment of one of Egypt's gods.

For instance, the Egyptians worshiped the Nile River, so God turned it into blood! They worshipped frogs, so God made sure they had plenty of frog legs to eat! There was such a plague of frogs that the creatures got into their houses, their beds, and their food!

Exodus 12:12

12 For I will pass through the land of Egypt this night, and will smite all the firstborn in the land of Egypt, both man and beast; AND AGAINST ALL THE GODS OF EGYPT I WILL EXECUTE JUDGEMENT: I am the Lord.

Numbers 33:4

4 For the Egyptians buried all their firstborn, which the Lord had smitten among them: UPON THEIR GODS ALSO THE LORD EXECUTED JUDGEMENTS.

The plague spoken of in this verse was the final blow. All the firstborn in Egypt would die! However, among the Israelite households, none would be hurt if they applied the blood of a sacrificed lamb to the doorposts of their houses. This sacrificed animal couldn't be just any lamb—it had to be a spotless, unblemished male. The blood of that lamb protected the Israelites from the judgment of God.

Exodus 12:2–8
2 This month shall be unto you the beginning of months: it shall
be the first month of the year to you.
3 Speak ye unto all the congregation of Israel, saying, In the
tenth day of this month they shall take to them every man a
lamb, according to the house of their fathers, a lamb for an
house:
4 And if the household be too little for the lamb, let him and
his neighbour next unto his house take it according to the
number of the souls; every man according to his eating shall
make your count for the lamb.
5 Your lamb shall be without blemish, a male of the first year:
ye shall take it out from the sheep, or from the goats:
6 And ye shall keep it up until the fourteenth day of the same
month: and the whole assembly of the congregation of Israel
shall kill it in the evening.
7 And they shall take of the blood, and strike it on the two side
posts and on the upper door post of the houses, wherein they
shall eat it.
8 And they shall eat the flesh in that night, roast with fire, and
unleavened bread; and with bitter herbs they shall eat it.

Now let me interject a thought here. Let us move ahead in time to when Jesus Christ was about to die as the Lamb of God. As He predicted His death in just a few days, He said this:

John 12:31
31 Now is the judgment of this world: now shall the prince of
this world be cast out.

And Jesus said a little while later of the Holy Spirit:

John 16:8–11
8 And when he is come, he will reprove the world of sin, and of
righteousness, and of judgment:

9 Of sin, because they believe not on me;
10 Of righteousness, because I go to my Father, and ye see me no more;
11 Of judgment, BECAUSE THE PRINCE OF THIS WORLD IS JUDGED.

In the Bible, Egypt is a type or symbol of the world system dominated by Satan. When God judged the gods of Egypt and delivered His people through the blood of the lamb, He was pointing to the future time when His Son Jesus would die as the Lamb of God. And when Jesus took the judgment of God upon Himself in our place, in so doing He brought God's judgment on the devil.

Later the Apostle Paul said the devil did not understand what God would do through Jesus' sacrifice.

1 Corinthians 2:8
8 Which none of the princes of this world knew: for had they known it, they would not have crucified the Lord of glory.

Now let's go back to the Israelites. The blood signaled the Israelites' deliverance from Egypt. The Lord's judgment fell on the gods of Egypt, and the Israelites left Egypt delivered, healthy, and prosperous once again!

Psalm 105:24,37
24 And he increased his people greatly; and made them stronger than their enemies....
37 He brought them forth also with silver and gold: and there was not one feeble person among their tribes.

These verses tell us that the Israelites left Egypt blessed—not weak, sick, and poor.

As I mention Israel's prosperity, I want to explain something about a peculiar instruction God gave the Israelites before they left Egypt.

Did you ever wonder why God told the Israelites to "borrow" from their Egyptian neighbors?

Exodus 3:21–22
21 And I will give this people favour in the sight of the Egyptians: and it shall come to pass, that, when ye go, ye shall not go empty:
22 But every woman shall borrow of her neighbour, and of her that sojourneth in her house, jewels of silver, and jewels of gold, and raiment: and ye shall put them upon your sons, and upon your daughters; and ye shall spoil the Egyptians.

When the Israelites "borrowed" those items from the Egyptians, it almost appears that they were stealing from them, since they knew they were about to leave Egypt. But let us take a closer look at this. Where did the Egyptians get their wealth in the first place?

In Genesis chapter 41 we read that Joseph, one of the sons of Jacob, interpreted Pharaoh's dream and was made ruler over all Egypt. Joseph was Pharaoh's chief administrator during the seven prosperous years that preceded seven years of famine. By the end of the years of famine, the Egyptians had sold their land, their possessions, and even themselves as slaves to Pharaoh in order to buy food from Joseph so they could survive (see Genesis 47:17–22). Notice in particular the following verse.

Genesis 47:23
23 Then Joseph said unto the people, Behold, I have bought you this day and your land for Pharaoh: lo, here is seed for you, and ye shall sow the land.

This verse shows that the Egyptians had sold themselves and their land to Joseph and Pharaoh. But a few verses later we see another group of people who had not sold all their possessions during the seven years of famine.

Genesis 47:27
27 And Israel dwelt in the land of Egypt, in the country of Goshen; and they had possessions therein, and grew, and multiplied exceedingly.

Apart from the government of Egypt and the Egyptian priests, no one owned anything in Egypt—that is, no one except the Israelites! They were the only free people there. All the rest were slaves to Pharaoh.

Then as we come down through history to a time some 400 years later, what do we see? The Israelites are slaves, and the Egyptians have the wealth and possessions. How do you suppose the Egyptians got that wealth?

Well, a new king, or pharaoh, arose over Egypt who did not know Joseph (Exod. 1:7–8). The king said, "*. . . Behold, the people of the children of Israel are* MORE AND MIGHTIER *than we*" (Exod. 1:9). So the Egyptians began to oppress and afflict the Israelites.

The Bible doesn't tell us the details of how the Israelites went from prosperity and freedom to poverty and slavery. The change probably began with the new king and authorities slowly passing laws to restrict the Israelites' freedoms and business dealings. They probably began to tax them more and more and bring legal challenges against them in the courts until their property was confiscated, their wealth plundered, and their freedom gone.

The Egyptians stole the possessions, positions, and prosperity of the children of Israel. So when God told the Israelites in Exodus chapter 3 to take their neighbors' wealth, the Israelites weren't stealing it. They were taking back what had been stolen from them!

Egypt is a type or symbol of the world system, and pharaoh is a type of Satan. For those of us who have made Jesus Christ our Savior and Lord, the blood of Jesus is our deliverance from slavery to the world.

Israel applied the blood of lambs to the doorposts of their houses, and when judgment came they were protected. God had already destined judgment for Egypt, and He didn't want His people partaking of that judgment. The blood of the lamb on the doorposts of the house was God's "proof-of-purchase" seal. He was saying to the destroyer, "These are My people. Don't touch them!" God told Israel, *". . . When I see the blood, I will pass over you, and the plague shall not be upon you to destroy you . . ."*(Exod. 12:13).

Although God sent the judgments upon Egypt, He Himself was not doing the actual work but had turned loose "the destroyer" upon them. In John chapter 10, the Bible calls Satan the destroyer.

John 10:10
10 The thief cometh not, but for to steal, and to kill, and to destroy: I am come that they might have life, and that they might have it more abundantly.

In the midst of the destruction God was sending upon the Egyptians, He wanted to make sure His people were protected.

Exodus 12:23

23 For the Lord will pass through to smite the Egyptians; and when he seeth the blood upon the lintel, and on the two side posts, the Lord will pass over the door, and will not suffer the destroyer to come in unto your houses to smite you.

The Lord was saying that when He saw the blood, He Himself would "pass over" that house as a protective covering and not allow the destroyer to touch them!

Similarly, when we surrender our lives to Jesus Christ, the blood that He shed for us on the Cross is applied to our hearts and lives. We become His property—separated from the world and the judgments to come.

When the destroyer passed through Egypt to kill the firstborn of all families, by right, the Israelites should also have suffered. But in reality, the lamb died in their place. You see, the wages of sin is death (Rom. 6:23), and the presence of sin demands judgment. When God saw the blood of the lamb on the door of an Israelite's house, He saw that the price for sin had already been paid. Therefore, the destroyer could not touch them!

Even though the family members inside the house were imperfect and had no righteousness of themselves, yet the blood of the lamb kept them from the destroyer and the judgment!

The sacrifice of the lambs, like all the other animal sacrifices made under the Old Covenant, was a temporary measure employed to pay for Israel's sins. You could say the Israelites were borrowing their forgiveness and righteousness on credit until Jesus Christ could make the final "balloon payment" on the loan through His death and resurrection. That is when God paid off the whole debt of the sins of mankind through the blood of the only perfect Lamb—Jesus, the Anointed Son of God!

Under the Old Covenant, every time an animal was sacrificed, God was saying to the demands of the perfect holy Law that required payment for sin, "Charge it to My account for now. I will be paying off the whole bill soon!" Glory to God!

So Old Testament saints were saved "on credit"—they were looking to the future for the perfect Sacrifice to come.

Hebrews 11:39–40
39 And these all, having obtained a good report through faith,
received not the promise:
40 God having provided some better thing for us, that they
without us should not be made perfect.

So the Old Testament saints had to wait for the perfect Lamb of God to be sacrificed so they could be "made perfect." Look at what their condition has become since Christ came:

Hebrews 12:22–24
22 But ye are come unto mount Sion, and unto the city of the
living God, the heavenly Jerusalem, and to an innumerable
company of angels,
23 To the general assembly and church of the firstborn, which
are written in heaven, and to God the Judge of all, AND TO THE
SPIRITS OF JUST MEN MADE PERFECT,
24 And to Jesus the mediator of the new covenant, and to the
blood of sprinkling, that speaketh better things than that
of Abel.

Referring to the Old Testament saints, the writer calls them "the spirits of just men made perfect." New Testament believers are called "the general assembly and church of the firstborn."

This is a subject all in itself and we won't go into detail about it here, except to say this: All those who died in faith under the Old Testament were looking toward the future sacrifice. After they died, they waited in a place the Scriptures call "Abraham's bosom" (Luke 16:22). It wasn't until Jesus was raised from the dead that they were made perfect through His sacrifice and taken to Heaven with Him. (For more on this subject see Matthew 27:52–53 and Ephesians 4:8.)

Jesus came to earth and sacrificed His life for us, paying off our debt of sin. Since that time we are not saved "on credit"; The record of our debt has been stamped "PAID IN FULL"! The price that Jesus paid—His perfect, sinless blood—was enough to take care of all the past debt of sin, plus any sins to come until the end of time.

Old Testament saints looked to the future, but we as New Testament believers look back to the Cross.

What Jesus did on the Cross landed a "one-two punch" against the devil and his works in our lives. Number one: the devil can't touch us because he has no right to. Jesus has paid for our sin, as the Bible tells us in the following verses.

Colossians 2:13–15
13 And you, being dead in your sins and the uncircumcision of your flesh, hath he quickened together with him, having forgiven you all trespasses;
14 Blotting out the handwriting of ordinances that was against us, which was contrary to us, and took it out of the way, nailing it to his cross;
15 And having spoiled principalities and powers, he made a shew of them openly, triumphing over them in it.

Romans 5:8–9
8 But God commendeth his love toward us, in that, while we were yet sinners, Christ died for us.
9 Much more then, being now justified by his blood, we shall be saved from wrath through him.

Understand this: In His life Jesus took our place and fulfilled the requirements of the Law for us. He obeyed in our place. In His death He took on Himself, in our place, the consequences of breaking the law! He fulfilled the law in His life and took the "curse of the law" in His death (Gal. 3:13).

Because Jesus Christ met all the requirements, God is able to accept us in Jesus as righteous, and that means the devil no longer has any authority over us! The charges that were against us have been taken away!

The second punch that Jesus landed on the devil at the Cross was to make us God's property. We now belong to God.

1 Corinthians 6:19–20
19 What? know ye not that your body is the temple of the Holy Ghost which is in you, which ye have of God, and ye are not your own?
20 For ye are bought with a price: therefore glorify God in your body, and in your spirit, which are God's.

Through the redemption process God purchased us at the price of the blood of His Son! This is what salvation is all about. You are putting your trust in Jesus' blood as final payment for your sins. He took upon Himself the judgment that we deserved. And Jesus not only paid for our sins; He bought us. We are now His property!

1 Peter 1:18–20
18 Forasmuch as ye know that ye were not redeemed with corruptible things, as silver and gold, from your vain conversation received by tradition from your fathers;
19 But with the precious blood of Christ, as of a lamb without blemish and without spot:
20 Who verily was foreordained before the foundation of the world, but was manifest in these last times for you.

The blood of a lamb *separated the Israelites from their past*—from slavery and bondage. God told them that the month the Passover was observed would be for them the beginning of their new year.

Exodus 12:1–2
1 And the Lord spake unto Moses and Aaron in the land of Egypt, saying,
2 This month shall be unto you the beginning of months: it shall be the first month of the year to you.

God instituted a new calendar for them, based on their deliverance from Egypt. They weren't even to associate with the past calendar! It was a completely new beginning!

When you put your trust in Jesus Christ's sacrifice and are "born again," you have a new calendar also! A new beginning!

2 Corinthians 5:17
17 Therefore if any man be in Christ, he is a new creature: old things are passed away; behold, all things are become new.

Now look at Hebrews chapter 9.

Hebrews 9:14
14 HOW MUCH MORE shall the blood of Christ, who through the eternal Spirit offered himself without spot to God, purge your conscience from dead works to serve the living God?

The Old Testament sacrifices were a temporary putting away of the remembrance of sin, but the blood of Christ cleanses our conscience! The conscience is where the memory of failure (guilt) paralyzes mankind and keeps them from walking in all of their God-given potential.

When Adam and Eve sinned in the Garden of Eden they

were ashamed because their nakedness became known to them. In their guilt they were afraid of God and hid from Him. They tried to cover their shame by sewing fig leaves together for clothing. After God dealt with both them and the serpent that deceived them, He had to do something about the fig leaves. You see, leaves make poor clothing. They wear out very fast and won't last in the environmental conditions. So what was God's solution? He covered them with animal skins!

> **Genesis 3:21**
> **21** Unto Adam also and to his wife did the Lord God make coats of skins, and clothed them.

What this means is that two animals had to die to cover their sin! Blood was shed.

> **Hebrews 9:22**
> **22** And almost all things are by the law purged with blood; and without shedding of blood is no remission.

The fig leaves represent man's efforts to deal with sin. This is called "religion." It will never work. God Himself had to provide the sacrifice.

Just before He clothed Adam and Eve with the skins, God spoke the first prophecy in the Bible of the coming Lamb of God:

> **Genesis 3:15**
> **15** And I will put enmity between thee and the woman, and between thy seed and her seed; it shall bruise thy head, and thou shalt bruise his heel.

This is the first recorded Messianic prophecy of the coming One. He would be born of a virgin (the seed of the woman, not the seed of man) and would crush the devil's head, though He himself would suffer a fatal strike on the heel.

It was through Jesus' death and resurrection that He defeated the devil and provided the solution to the problem of man's sin.

Praise God! When we put our faith in the Lamb of God and His blood, we are cleansed from all the effects of sin and failure—past, present, and (praise God!) future. The blood of Jesus is constantly speaking in the present tense before God's throne in Heaven (Heb. 12:24).

God is the great I AM (Exod. 3:14). And when we believe First John 1:9, the ever-present cleansing of the blood of Jesus is immediately available to us.

1 John 1:9
9 If we confess our sins, he is faithful and just to forgive us our sins, and to cleanse us from all unrighteousness.

Hebrews 13:20–21
20 Now the God of peace, that brought again from the dead our Lord Jesus, that great shepherd of the sheep, THROUGH THE BLOOD of the everlasting covenant,
21 Make you perfect in every good work to do his will, working in you that which is wellpleasing in his sight, through Jesus Christ; to whom be glory for ever and ever. Amen.

Through the blood of Jesus, God is able to make us completely whole people and work in our lives the good things He desires.

chapter 4

Through the Flood

Moreover, brethren, I would not that ye should be ignorant, how that all our fathers were under the cloud, and all passed through the sea; And were all baptized unto Moses in the cloud and in the sea.

—1 Corinthians 10:1–2

When the Israelites left Egypt, the cloud of God's Presence covered them and lead them along the way. That cloud led them up to and through the Red Sea. The Bible says Israel was "baptized unto Moses" in the cloud and in the sea.

In this chapter I would like us to consider the Israelites' passing through the Red Sea.

As they approached the sea, the children of Israel had left Egypt and had been freed from slavery, but Pharaoh was chasing them to try to put them back under bondage.

Exodus 14:5

5 And it was told the king of Egypt that the people fled: and the heart of Pharaoh and of his servants was turned against the people, and they said, Why have we done this, that we have let Israel go from serving us?

As Israel journeyed to the Red Sea, Pharaoh and his army were in pursuit. Israel's past was chasing them. This is exactly what the devil tries to do to us once we have been freed from his control over us. He tries to put us back into bondage! The Word of God calls Satan "the accuser of our brethren" (Rev. 12:10). He will try to haunt us with our past to keep us from enjoying the promises of God.

The Israelites' past was trying to drag them back. But Moses said, *". . . the Egyptians whom ye have seen to day, ye shall see them again no more for ever"* (Exod. 14:13). You see, the journey through the Red Sea was symbolic of the children of Israel being baptized unto Moses. It symbolized the Israelites' separation from the past. When the Israelites passed through the waters of the Red Sea, it marked freedom from the old world in which they had lived.

Israel had been delivered! They entered the sea and came out on the other side into a new world. They stepped onto new ground.

The Egyptians represented the judgment, bondage, condemnation, and sin that were trying to follow them. But the waters of the sea swallowed up the Egyptians (see Exod. 14:21–28). The past could not follow Israel through the flood onto that new ground.

And that new ground was shouting ground! They had a "praise meeting" right there on the beach! They stepped onto the shoreline and watched the same flood that brought salvation for them bring judgment on the world. When the Red Sea closed up behind the Israelites, it closed the door on their past.

What happened to the children of Israel at the Red Sea is a picture of the deliverance we as Christians have in Jesus Christ. When the Israelites stepped over onto the other shore, they stepped into a new world of freedom. In the same way, we have been delivered in Christ! Through our redemption in Him, we have stepped into a new world of freedom.

Colossians 1:12–14
12 Giving thanks unto the Father, which hath made us meet [or able] to be partakers of the inheritance of the saints in light:
13 Who hath delivered us from the power of darkness, and hath translated us into the kingdom of his dear Son:
14 In whom we have redemption through his blood, even the forgiveness of sins . . . .

The "baptism unto Moses" that the Israelites experienced at the Red Sea is a picture, or type, of the Church being baptized into Christ and delivered from the world, the devil, and sin.

Romans 6:3–11
3 Know ye not, that so many of us as were baptized into Jesus Christ were baptized into his death?
4 Therefore we are buried with him by baptism into death: that like as Christ was raised up from the dead by the glory of the Father, even so we also should walk in newness of life.
5 For if we have been planted together in the likeness of his death, we shall be also in the likeness of his resurrection:
6 Knowing this, that our old man is crucified with him, that the body of sin might be destroyed, that henceforth we should not serve sin.
7 For he that is dead is freed from sin.
8 Now if we be dead with Christ, we believe that we shall also live with him:
9 Knowing that Christ being raised from the dead dieth no more; death hath no more dominion over him.
10 For in that he died, he died unto sin once: but in that he liveth, he liveth unto God.
11 Likewise reckon ye also yourselves to be dead indeed unto sin, but alive unto God through Jesus Christ our Lord.

As we will see in our next illustration, in the Scriptures water sometimes symbolizes death or judgment. Christ died under the judgment of God in our place—taking our sin upon Himself.

Isaiah 53:3–6
3 He is despised and rejected of men; a man of sorrows, and acquainted with grief: and we hid as it were our faces from him; he was despised, and we esteemed him not.
4 Surely he hath borne our griefs, and carried our sorrows: yet we did esteem him stricken, smitten of God, and afflicted.
5 But he was wounded for our transgressions, he was bruised for our iniquities: the chastisement of our peace was upon him; and with his stripes we are healed.
6 All we like sheep have gone astray; we have turned every one to his own way; and the Lord hath laid on him the iniquity of us all.

Now look at another verse in that same chapter:

Isaiah 53:10
10 Yet it pleased the Lord to bruise him; he hath put him to grief: when thou shalt make his soul an offering for sin, he shall see his seed, he shall prolong his days, and the pleasure of the Lord shall prosper in his hand.

The New Testament says that Jesus "became sin for us" (2 Cor. 5:21) and was made "a curse for us" (Gal. 3:13). He died under the waters of judgment for us. Jesus alluded to this in referring to His own death when He said to two of His disciples, *"Ye know not what ye ask: can ye drink of the cup that I drink of? and be baptized with the baptism that I am baptized with?"* (Mark 10:38). Jesus' baptism in the Jordan River at the beginning of His ministry was a symbol of the actual baptism He would experience in His death.

Now let's look at another illustration, another Bible story that reveals this same truth. When Noah and his family went into the ark God had him build, they were delivered through the flood from their past (Genesis chapters 6–9). The flood meant judgment for the wicked, but it meant salvation for the eight people in the ark. They were delivered into a new world.

In the story of Noah's ark, we find a marvelous example to help us understand the finished work of Christ and what it means to us as believers. The Old Testament was given to us as an example. We can study the stories of the Old Testament and apply what we learn from them to our lives today.

1 Corinthians 10:11
11 Now all these things happened unto them for ensamples: and they are written for our admonition, upon whom the ends of the world are come.

When God directed Noah to build the ark, He was very specific. In other words, God told Noah the exact dimensions to which to build it and how many animals to gather into it. And He told him to seal the ark with pitch.

Genesis 6:14
14 Make thee an ark of gopher wood; rooms shalt thou make in the ark, and shalt PITCH it within and without with PITCH.

This is very significant. The word "pitch" is translated from the Hebrew word *kopher*, which can also be translated "cover." It is also the identical word for "atonement"! The Lord was showing us that those inside the ark would be protected by the Atonement!

Noah's ark, of course, gives us an example of what we are discussing in this book: our separation from the old life and our coming into the new. The ark was a symbol of death to those outside of it, because everyone outside the ark died. And the ark was a symbol of Christ to those on the inside, because the ark protected those on the inside from the judgment of God.

The ark is an example of our death, burial, and resurrection in Christ. It represented the Body of Christ.

> **Romans 7:4**
> **4** Wherefore, my brethren, ye also are become dead to the law BY THE BODY OF CHRIST; that ye should be married to another, even to him who is raised from the dead, that we should bring forth fruit unto God.

> **Colossians 1:20–22**
> **20** And, having made peace through the blood of his cross, by him to reconcile all things unto himself; by him, I say, whether they be things in earth, or things in heaven.
> **21** And you, that were sometime alienated and enemies in your mind by wicked works, yet now hath he reconciled
> **22** IN THE BODY OF HIS FLESH THROUGH DEATH, to present you holy and unblameable and unreproveable in his sight . . . .

Have you, like many others, seen an artist's drawing or rendering of Noah's ark? Some researchers in recent times have even claimed to have seen the evidence of the ark on Mount Ararat and have said that, rather than being shaped like a ship, it was shaped like a long box or, if you will, a coffin. From the dimensions given in the Bible, it appears to have been shaped like a long box.

When the floods came, the water became a symbol of judgment and death to those on the outside. To those inside the ark, the water became a symbol of the death of their past life, just like water baptism is a symbol to us of the death of our past life.

This is why we are baptized in water after becoming Christians. This is why water baptism is an important part of the Gospel. I've heard traditional churches say that the reason for baptism is for a public "testimony" of our faith. Undoubtedly, it is, but it is more than that! Water baptism is meant to be for the benefit of the one being baptized. It is a funeral for your "old" self.

When someone has passed away, the funeral service is the point of finality—when the reality "sinks in" that the person is gone permanently. The funeral service helps people deal with this finality and go on with their new life without the person who passed away.

When you came to Christ, your old self died. Water baptism is a way for you to cut off your association with the past; it serves as the funeral for your old self. The one big difference is that you aren't mourning the loss of your old life but are rejoicing that it is gone!

Some non-Christian cultures understand this fact better than the Church does. In these cultures, if one is converted to Christianity, for example, and is baptized, the family will cut them off—disown them—and say that their son or daughter who became a Christian is dead. The family will actually hold a funeral service for their loved one who became a Christian!

There is too little emphasis placed on the importance of water baptism in some segments of the Church today. It is true that certain denominations teach that you aren't saved if you are not baptized in water, or if you haven't been baptized with their "patented formula." Those groups are missing the whole picture of what we are discussing here.

On the other hand, you have a lot of churches that don't emphasize water baptism at all. What I can see from my own experience, and that of many others, is that when a person is truly born again and properly instructed in water baptism, and then he is baptized, he seems to make a clean break with his past. I believe this is what Peter meant when he said the following.

> **1 Peter 3:21**
> **21** The like figure whereunto even baptism doth also now save us (not the putting away of the filth of the flesh, but the answer of a good conscience toward God,) by the resurrection of Jesus Christ.

It is not the physical washing of water baptism that helps us, but the effect that baptism has on our conscience. Remember, God does not institute certain practices just to fill up our time with religious activities. What He tells us to do is important for us and helps us grow in Christ.

For us to understand the various types of baptisms mentioned in the New Testament, it is important to consider these things:

Who is doing the baptizing?

What is the person being baptized into?

When a person becomes a Christian and is baptized in water, the person doing the baptizing is a minister, and the element in which the person is baptized is water. The act of water baptism symbolizes the person's death, burial, and resurrection in Christ.

The Bible also says that a person who becomes a Christian is baptized *into* the Body of Christ *by* the Holy Spirit, making him part of the Church (1 Cor. 12:13). The Holy Spirit is the One doing the baptizing, and the element into which the person is being baptized is the Body of Christ.

However, there is another baptism for the Christian—the baptism in the Holy Spirit. Here Jesus is doing the baptizing and the Holy Spirit is the element into which the believer is baptized. Consider the words of John the Baptist as recorded in Matthew chapter 3:

> **Matthew 3:11**
> **11** I indeed baptize you with water unto repentance: but he that cometh after me is mightier than I, whose shoes I am not worthy to bear: he shall baptize you with the Holy Ghost, and with fire.

One way to look at this is, when we are saved the Holy Spirit introduces us to Jesus and makes us a part of His Body. When we are baptized in the Holy Spirit, Jesus introduces us to the Third Person of the Trinity.

You might say, "What about Ephesians 4:5 where it says there is only one baptism?"

I'm glad you asked! The answer, as always, is 'context.' What is the context of the passage?

Ephesians was written to Gentile (non-Jewish) believers to show them who they were, what they had, and what had been done to them in Christ. Then the writer, the Apostle Paul, showed them that they were not a separate Body of Christ from the Jews; they were part of the same Body. Look at the context:

Ephesians 2:11–19
11 Wherefore remember, that ye being in time past Gentiles in the flesh, who are called Uncircumcision by that which is called the Circumcision in the flesh made by hands;
12 That at that time ye were without Christ, being aliens from the commonwealth of Israel, and strangers from the covenants of promise, having no hope, and without God in the world:
13 But now in Christ Jesus ye who sometimes were far off are made nigh by the blood of Christ.
14 For he is our peace, who hath made both one, and hath broken down the middle wall of partition between us;
15 Having abolished in his flesh the enmity, even the law of commandments contained in ordinances; for to make in himself of twain one new man, so making peace;
16 And that he might reconcile both unto God in one body by the cross, having slain the enmity thereby:
17 And came and preached peace to you which were afar off, and to them that were nigh.
18 For through him we both have access by one Spirit unto the Father.
19 Now therefore ye are no more strangers and foreigners, but fellowcitizens with the saints, and of the household of God . . . .

Look at the word *one* in verses 14–16 above. *One* refers to there being one Body of Christ. There are not separate Gentile and Jewish Churches or Bodies. Then in verse 18, Paul says there is only One Spirit. There is not a Jewish Holy Spirit and a Gentile Holy Spirit.

In Chapter 3 Paul says that the mystery from ages past was that the Gentiles would be part of the same Body with the Jews:

Ephesians 3:4–6
4 (Whereby, when ye read, ye may understand my knowledge in the mystery of Christ)
5 Which in other ages was not made known unto the sons of men, as it is now revealed unto his holy apostles and prophets by the Spirit;
6 That the Gentiles should be fellowheirs, and of the same body, and partakers of his promise in Christ by the gospel . . . .

Now go to Chapter 4. Paul exhorted them to "keep the unity of the Spirit in the bond of peace." Then he said:

Ephesians 4:4–6
4 There is one body, and one Spirit, even as ye are called in one hope of your calling;
5 One Lord, one faith, one baptism,
6 One God and Father of all, who is above all, and through all, and in you all.

The baptism mentioned in verse 5 is our baptism by the Holy Spirit into the Body of Christ when we were saved! It is the same baptism for Jew and Gentile alike. There is only one baptism by the Holy Spirit into Christ's Body. There are not two different baptisms.

The Apostle Paul could have said it this way: "It is the same Body, the same Spirit, the same Lord, the same faith, and the same baptism." He was not saying there is only one kind of baptism. The Scriptures speak plainly of baptism in water, baptism in the Body of Christ, and baptism in the Holy Spirit.

If you are a Christian and have never experienced water baptism, I encourage you to talk with a Bible-believing minister about it and pursue it. (I'm not referring to a religious ceremony you may have been part of when you were younger, before you were saved.) Water baptism is an outward act of faith in the inward work of the Cross. It shows that your old life was crucified with Christ. It died with Him and, was buried with Him, and you rose from the dead with Him to a new life.

We will look more into the work of the Holy Spirit in Chapter 6 of this book. But now I would like to return to our discussion of Noah's ark. We can see that the ark, like water baptism, symbolizes our burial with Christ. We know that the contents of the ark were protected, even though the ark itself experienced the outpouring of God's wrath.

The past lives of those inside the ark were buried under the water as judgment was poured out on the earth. The raging waters tossed the ark to and fro, but the rain stopped, the flood waters receded, and those inside came forth into a new world free from the judgments of the past.

This is exactly what Christ did for us as He carried us in His heart to the Cross! He bore the judgment of God upon Himself for the sins of mankind and went under the "waters of death" so we could be delivered into a new world, free from the past.

There is a paraphrase of the New Testament in contemporary language titled *The Message*. Romans 6:1–3 in this version shows explicitly what I am saying:

Romans 6:1–3 (*The Message*)
So what do we do? Keep on sinning so God can keep on forgiving?
I should hope not! If we've left the country where sin is sovereign, how can we still live in our old house there?
Or didn't you realize we packed up and left there for good? That is what happened in baptism. When we went under the water, we left the old country of sin behind; when we came up out of the water, we entered into the new country of grace—a new life in a new land!

When we are in Christ, we not only partake of the death and burial of Christ, but also the resurrection of Christ and all the benefits that go along with it!

Just as those eight souls who were in the ark left their past behind them when God shut the door, so, when we accept Jesus Christ as our personal Savior, God shuts the door on our past.

Genesis 7:16
16 And they that went in, went in male and female of all flesh, as God had commanded him: and THE LORD SHUT HIM IN.

If you are in Christ, you have no past. If you could use the computers of Heaven to investigate the history of your life before you became a Christian, all you would find is a screen that reads, "No Records Found"! When you entered into Christ, God shut the door on your past!

When those eight souls came out of that ark several months later, they entered a new world! When that door opened up, they saw the rainbow and the sunshine and a new creation. Their past was gone forever. The evil of the previous world was gone!

It's just the same when we accept Jesus as our Savior and our Lord. The record of our past is wiped away. We're made new creatures in Christ Jesus, and we begin living a new life in Christ.

chapter 5

The Ghost of Pharaoh

So far we have seen two different symbols, or types, of our salvation through Jesus Christ. First, we looked at the children of Israel's deliverance from Egypt through the blood of a spotless lamb and through the flood of the Red Sea. The lamb's blood applied to the doorposts of the Israelites' houses in Egypt pointed to the blood of the sinless Lamb of God shed for us at Calvary. The flood of the Red Sea looked ahead to our baptism into the Body of Christ. Second, we looked at Noah and his family and their deliverance from the past through the "covering atonement" on the ark, which carried them through the flood. This pointed to Christ carrying us in His heart to the Cross. We died with Him, were buried with Him, and rose again with Him to new life.

Let the reality of these truths sink into your mind. Realizing what has happened to you through the New Birth will do away with a lot of nonsense some people go through trying to deal with their past!

There is a lot of good in dealing with the past in the area of forgiveness. We all need to learn to forgive those who have hurt us. We need to not carry around grudges all of our lives about things that happened years ago. I have seen people take unforgiveness with them right to the grave. It made their lives miserable on earth, destroyed their health, and finally killed them. If you are born again, you have the ability to forgive. You are *commanded* to forgive! It is part of your new life in Christ.

The only areas of our past that I see the New Testament telling us to deal with are forgiveness, and sometimes restitution. Jesus said that unforgiveness would hinder our faith (Mark 11:24–25). He also told a parable about a servant whose master forgave him of a large debt (Matt. 18:22–35). The servant could not repay the debt, so his master forgave it. (Notice that the servant *was not able* to repay this debt. The parallel to our situation is that, before we accepted Jesus as our Savior, we owed a debt of sin that was impossible for us to pay.)

After being forgiven of his large debt, this servant then found a fellow servant who owed him a small debt. But unlike his master, he did not forgive his fellow servant his debt. Instead, he demanded payment. When the fellow servant said he needed time to pay back the debt, the unforgiving servant had him thrown in jail.

When the master found out what had happened, he called in the unforgiving servant and reinstated his debt:

Matthew 18:34–35
34 And his lord was wroth, and delivered him to the tormentors, till he should pay all that was due unto him.
35 So likewise shall my heavenly Father do also unto you, if ye from your hearts forgive not every one his brother their trespasses.

There's a serious lesson here. Unforgiveness actually caused the reinstatement of the servant's previously forgiven debt. And he would suffer torment until it was paid.

Though Jesus Christ has paid for the curse of the law, the effects of that curse—sickness, poverty, and other negative things—could still operate in a Christian's life if that Christian is in unforgiveness!

If someone offends you, get back under grace! Forgive those who offend you and let the offense go!

Unforgiveness brings torment to people's lives! If you have not forgiven someone for something they did in the past, you had better do it. You are commanded to forgive. Unforgiveness seems to be the one thing that can tie you to your past. But it doesn't have to!

To not forgive someone for something they did to you is to say they "owe" you something. Have you ever heard someone say, "So-and-so owes me an apology!" You are saying that someone owes you a debt and you won't forgive that debt but expect full payment for it. The offender must "do" something to pay you back, or make up for what they have done to you.

Actually, the Bible says *you* owe *them*!

Romans 13:8–10

8 Owe no man any thing, but to love one another: for he that loveth another hath fulfilled the law.

9 For this, Thou shalt not commit adultery, Thou shalt not kill, Thou shalt not steal, Thou shalt not bear false witness, Thou shalt not covet; and if there be any other commandment, it is briefly comprehended in this saying, namely, Thou shalt love thy neighbour as thyself.

10 Love worketh no ill to his neighbour: therefore love is the fulfilling of the law.

Listen! If God forgave you your entire debt of sin that was impossible for you to pay, what right do you have to demand that someone pay you back for some offense they may have committed against you?

According to the Bible, the person who holds another accountable to them for their offenses will end up paying for their own debt of sin, and being tormented while doing so. The tormentor has wreaked destruction in many believers' lives because they refused to forgive. Sickness, disease, sorrows, and even death are the price one pays for unforgiveness. It is not worth it!

If you will forgive those who have hurt you, the past cannot keep you.

Concerning the past, many Christians are trying to go back to the days before they became a new creation and fix their past. You cannot fix it. Why? Because in the eyes of God there is nothing to fix! You must realize that the past is gone and stop allowing the influence of the former life to dominate your life now.

Trying to fix your old life is like putting new wine into old wineskins.

Luke 5:37–38
37 And no man putteth new wine into old bottles; else the new wine will burst the bottles, and be spilled, and the bottles shall perish.
38 But new wine must be put into new bottles; and both are preserved.

In Bible days people could not put brand new wine into an old wineskin. (The *King James Version* calls wineskins "bottles.") As the new wine fermented, it would expand and burst the old skin.

You can't take the life of God and put it into your old fixed-up self. Your old self couldn't handle it. No—God makes you "a new creature," "born again" . . . a new wineskin. When you became a Christian, the old wineskin of your old human nature was done away with.

I want to expound on something here for a moment. Some people, in the name of education, will charge you a lot of money to sit in their office week after week and relive all the hurt, pain, rejection, and bitterness of the past. This, they claim, brings inner healing.

But have you ever had a sore on your body that got better the more you picked at it? No! Your doctor probably told you to leave it alone and let it heal!

The soul of man is not much different from the body in this matter. Time and forgiveness are the best treatments.

Now if you are in a state of denial, ignoring your unforgiveness, bitterness, or hurts, you need to face them, confess them to God, and forgive others. Then God can begin to work on your situation.

In such a case, a person may need counseling to help him face certain issues of the past and deal with them scripturally. But that doesn't mean watching "reruns" in his mind day after day and blaming his life's condition on the past.

The catch-all word of this generation is "dysfunctional." People are blaming all of their woes and current problems on a dysfunctional family life. Without a doubt, the breakup of the family in our society is taking its toll. I know that from personal experience as a youngster. But if we are going to claim to be Christians who believe that the Bible is God's Word to us, then how can we believe that our generation is more terrible than the Bible is powerful? How can we say that our problems are too difficult for God to solve? Why do we substitute man-made ideas and methods to deal with problems instead of believing God for the answers?

I'll tell you why. It's because it is easier for us to try some method that will make people feel sorry for us than it is to believe God for His forgiving and healing power!

I am convinced that a lot of the nonsense that goes on today to "deal with the past" is nothing more than a substitute for an old-fashioned, power-of-God revival in a person's life.

We should not be looking backward to the time before we were born again. We should be looking forward to the development of the new creation God has made us to be.

Trying to go back and fix your old life is like digging up a dead person and trying to heal them. Forget it! They are gone! And so is your old self.

We have been delivered from that old world and have become new creations. We need to get our minds renewed to the truth that we are new creatures and that we do not need to allow "Pharaoh and his Egyptians"—or, in other words, the devil—to chase us all over the desert trying to put us back in bondage.

Romans 12:1–2

1 I beseech you therefore, brethren, by the mercies of God, that ye present your bodies a living sacrifice, holy, acceptable unto God, which is your reasonable service.

2 And be not conformed to this world: but be ye transformed by the renewing of your mind, that ye may prove what is that good, and acceptable, and perfect, will of God.

What does the writer mean when he tells us in verse 1 to "present your bodies a living sacrifice"? He is simply saying that we have been crucified with Christ, buried with Him, and raised with Him to a new life. We are "dead" even though we still live.

Saint Paul put it this way:

Galatians 2:20
20 I am crucified with Christ: nevertheless I live; yet not I, but Christ liveth in me: and the life which I now live in the flesh I live by the faith of the Son of God, who loved me, and gave himself for me.

How do we renew our minds to this truth? We take a look in the mirror! . . . that is, the mirror of God's Word.

James 1:22–25
22 But be ye doers of the word, and not hearers only, deceiving your own selves.
23 For if any be a hearer of the word, and not a doer, he is like unto a man beholding his natural face in a glass [or mirror]:
24 For he beholdeth himself, and goeth his way, and straightway forgetteth what manner of man he was.
25 But whoso looketh into the perfect law of liberty, and continueth therein, he being not a forgetful hearer, but a doer of the work, this man shall be blessed in his deed.

I have heard some refer to these verses in the negative sense–saying that the mirror of the Word of God shows us our faults and we need to be reminded of them. Not so!

We are instructed to look at ourselves according to "the perfect law of liberty," not according to the law of sin, condemnation, and death! Verse 25 tells us that we are to continue in what we see. And what do we see when we look into this perfect law of liberty—God's Word? We see liberty and freedom!

Paul said the same thing a little differently:

2 Corinthians 3:17–18
17 Now the Lord is that Spirit: and where the Spirit of the Lord is, there is liberty.
18 But we all, with open face beholding as in a glass [or mirror] the glory of the Lord, are changed into the same image from glory to glory, even as by the Spirit of the Lord.

Paul said that as we keep looking into the mirror of God's Word we "behold" the glory of the Lord. As we continue to look, we are changed. James said that as we continue in what we see by putting what we see in the Word into practice, we are blessed in our works.

When we look into the Word of God, we don't see our old selves. We see who we are in Christ, what He has made us to be, and what He has given us.

It is as we continue to look at ourselves through the mirror of the Word that we begin to renew our minds and see ourselves the way God sees us in Christ.

When we look into a mirror, we see an image. As we look into the "mirror" of the Word of God, we see the image God has of us, not the image we have of ourselves. So often, the image we have of ourselves is one of defeat, bondage, sin, failure, sickness, lack, and every other negative thing.

No—in the mirror of God's Word, we see what *God* says about us. And He says we are saved, healed, made righteous and whole, His sons and daughters, children of the King!

As we continue in these things, we begin to see ourselves that way, and then we begin to act that way. Here is how Jesus said it:

John 8:31–32
31 . . . If ye continue in my word, then are ye my disciples indeed;
32 And ye shall know the truth, and the truth shall make you free.

There it is again—continue in the Word and the Truth will make you free! This is how we renew our minds to the powerful truths of God's Word.

Looking at this in a parallel way to the Israelites' deliverance from Egypt, the only thing that is chasing us now is Pharaoh's "ghost." For us to allow Satan to torment us with thoughts of things from our past would be like the children of Israel allowing Pharaoh's ghost to lie to them and chase them around the desert. Pharaoh was dead—buried in the Red Sea. He had no power over them any more. God had delivered them.

When I became a Christian my old life ceased to be—including my past involvement with the occult and the things of darkness. One night soon after I was saved, I had a dream that helped me see this. In my dream, I was standing in my parents' fenced-in back yard. (I was living with them at the time.) I heard a vicious dog barking on the other side of the fence, so I walked to the fence and looked over it. When I did, I saw a very vicious dog jumping up at me and trying to attack me. I quickly pulled back behind the protection of the fence.

My first reaction was fear. Then I looked over to my right and saw Jesus standing there looking at me with a peaceful expression on His face. Suddenly the fear was replaced with absolute peace. Then I awoke.

Immediately I knew what this dream meant. God was showing me that I was separated from my past and I did not have to be afraid of the devil. He could not touch me now. I was on the other side of the fence! I was now on God's side, in His kingdom!

Through the blood of the Lamb, the Lord Jesus Christ, we are saved from judgment and delivered from the world and from Pharaoh (the devil.) And our baptism in water becomes our personal "Red Sea" experience. We are showing outwardly what has happened inwardly. This is our "putting away" of the old life.

You are the righteousness of God in Christ!

You have the privilege of coming boldly before the Father! And you have this privilege not because of something you did or are going to do, but because of what Christ Jesus did for you at the Cross.

You have a new position!

You are someone special!

Your past is gone forever, and you are declared to be in right standing with God! Jesus took your judgment upon Himself. You've come out of the ark and have been delivered into a new Kingdom.

2 Corinthians 5:17

17 Therefore if any man be in Christ, he is a new creature: old things are passed away; behold, all things are become new.

We are forever separated from the past. We cannot go back. Noah and his family could no more get back into that ark and return to their old lives than we can return to our former life.

Some who have known Christ have acted as if they were living in their former lost condition. In reality they are children of God who are acting like the devil. As the Apostle Peter said, such a person ". . . *hath forgotten that he was purged from his old sins*" (2 Peter 1:9).

Such people are on dangerous ground and will have to give an account for their behavior. They are in danger of becoming what Jude calls " . . . *trees whose fruit withereth, without fruit, twice dead . . .* " (Jude 12).

I don't think this world has seen a more miserable person than one who has been delivered from his past and made to be a child of God, free from the devil's authority, yet has willingly gone back into the bondage of sin. Thank God, His mercy endureth forever, and the power of what He did for that person through Jesus is as able to deliver him from his backsliding as it was to free him from his past when he first believed!

God didn't want those eight people on the ark to be tempted to try to go back to what they had left behind. He wanted them to experience the blessings of the new life that was set before them. The wicked things they were delivered from in that old world were gone, forever! In the same way, the wicked things of our old life are gone—forever! *So don't try to climb back into the ark!*

chapter 6

Under the Cloud

Moreover, brethren, I would not that ye should be ignorant, how that all our fathers were under the cloud, and all passed through the sea; And were all baptized unto Moses in the cloud and in the sea.

—1 Corinthians 10:1–2

I would be leaving out of this book an important aspect of our deliverance from the past if I did not mention the involvement of the Holy Spirit. As you read the Old Testament account of Israel's deliverance from Egypt, you see that the visible manifestation of God's Presence—His Spirit—was with them from the very beginning in the form of a pillar of cloud.

Exodus 13:21–22
21 And the Lord went before them by day in A PILLAR OF A
CLOUD, to lead them the way; and by night in A PILLAR OF FIRE,
to give them light; to go by day and night:
22 He took not away the pillar of the cloud by day, nor the
pillar of fire by night, from before the people.

When the Bibles states, "The Lord went before them to lead them," it is referring to the pillar of cloud by day and the pillar of fire by night leading them in the way they should go. This is a perfect Old Testament picture of what the New Testament refers to as being led by the Spirit.

Romans 8:14
14 For as many as are led by the Spirit of God, they are the sons of God.

Galatians 5:18
18 But if ye be led of the Spirit, ye are not under the law.

The Egyptians did not have the cloud with them; only God's people did. The Jews have a name for the cloud. They call it the "Shekinah," which is the manifest Presence of God. It was this cloud of His Presence that came down upon Mount Sinai when God wrote the Law on the tablets of stone for Moses to bring to the people.

Exodus 19:9,16
9 And the Lord said unto Moses, Lo, I come unto thee in a thick cloud, that the people may hear when I speak with thee, and believe thee for ever. And Moses told the words of the people unto the Lord

16 And it came to pass on the third day in the morning, that there were thunders and lightnings, and A THICK CLOUD UPON THE MOUNT, and the voice of the trumpet exceeding loud; so that all the people that was in the camp trembled.

This was a picture of the New Testament Pentecost in Acts chapter 2 when the Holy Spirit came down as fire to write the laws of God in the hearts of men.

2 Corinthians 3:3
3 Forasmuch as ye are manifestly declared to be the epistle of Christ ministered by us, written not with ink, but with the Spirit

of the living God; not in tables of stone, but in fleshy tables of the heart.

Jeremiah 31:31–34
31 Behold, the days come, saith the Lord, that I will make a new covenant with the house of Israel, and with the house of Judah:
32 Not according to the covenant that I made with their fathers in the day that I took them by the hand to bring them out of the land of Egypt; which my covenant they brake, although I was an husband unto them, saith the Lord:
33 But this shall be the covenant that I will make with the house of Israel; After those days, saith the Lord, I will put my law in their inward parts, and write it in their hearts; and will be their God, and they shall be my people.
34 And they shall teach no more every man his neighbour, and every man his brother, saying, Know the Lord: for they shall all know me, from the least of them unto the greatest of them, saith the Lord; for I will forgive their iniquity, and I will remember their sin no more.

Ezekiel 36:26
26 A new heart also will I give you, and a new spirit will I put within you: and I will take away the stony heart out of your flesh, and I will give you an heart of flesh.

We see then that the Holy Spirit was very active in the deliverance of the people of God from Egypt, just as He is very active today in our deliverance from sin and the past.

Let us now look more closely at how the Holy Spirit helped the Israelites.

First of all, He led the children of Israel out of Egypt through the desert and right up to the Red Sea. There were mountains on either side of them, and the sea in front. This was a poor maneuver by military standards—so much so that Pharaoh said, " . . . They are trapped in the land; the wilderness has boxed them in" (Exod. 14:3), and he proceeded to pursue them.

Did God know what He was doing when He led the Israelites to this spot? The Israelites didn't think so. But what they thought was God's mistake and their destruction was really God's wisdom and the *enemy's* destruction! And God in His wisdom will do the same thing for us. Instead of letting us run from our past all of our lives, the Holy Spirit will lead us to situations where we must overcome and walk in victory. He will take us to places where our greatest weaknesses become opportunities for His greatest show of strength. He will help us face those areas of our lives that we want to ignore and pretend are not there.

For example, how many powerful men or women of God have you heard testify that, before God called them, they would be paralyzed with fear at the thought of speaking in front of people? How many preachers with a healing ministry have themselves been healed of some major physical problem? How many people who are able to minister effectively to the hearts of others have themselves been beset by heartache at some time? God did not put these troubles on them, but He led them to a place where they had to face them and overcome them. Remember, God is in the overcoming business!

It seems that most of the time in my own life, God has not led me by the most comfortable way. Instead, it seems He has caused me to face and overcome rejection, fears, and pain.

So in the account of Israel's escape from Egypt, what happened next? The cloud that had been in front of the people to lead them now went to the rear to protect them from Pharaoh who was chasing them!

Exodus 14:19–20

19 And the angel of God, which went before the camp of
Israel, removed and went behind them; and the pillar of the
cloud went from before their face, and stood behind them:
20 And it came between the camp of the Egyptians and the
camp of Israel; and it was a cloud and darkness to them, but it
gave light by night to these: so that the one came not near the
other all the night.

The pillar of cloud "insulated" the Israelites from the enemy. With unpleasant circumstances all around Israel and the enemy breathing down their necks, the Holy Spirit became a "force field" to protect them. He provided light and warmth to God's people but darkness and confusion to the enemy.

Verse 20 says, "*. . . so that the one came not near the other all the night.*" The Holy Spirit stood between the Israelites and Pharaoh's army all night long! In the same way, in our darkest hour the Holy Spirit will stand between us and the devil.

The Holy Spirit is the One Who will protect you from the past that tries to haunt you and keep you in failure. Praise God! The devil cannot get any closer to you than he can to the Presence of God!

1 John 4:4

4 Ye are of God, little children, and have overcome them:
because greater is he that is in you, than he that is in the world.

As a Spirit-filled New Testament believer, you have that Shekinah Presence, the Holy Spirit, inside you!

What other similarities can we see in this account in Exodus between what the Holy Spirit did for the Israelites and what He does for us today?

The pillar of cloud by day and the pillar of fire by night provided light and warmth. Light represents understanding, wisdom, and direction. The Israelites were able to travel at night because of the light (Exod. 13:21). Likewise, the Holy Spirit gives us direction and wisdom even in our darkest hour.

John 14:26
26 But the Comforter, which is the Holy Ghost, whom the Father will send in my name, he shall teach you all things, and bring all things to your remembrance, whatsoever I have said unto you.

John 16:13
13 Howbeit when he, the Spirit of truth, is come, he will guide you into all truth: for he shall not speak of himself; but whatsoever he shall hear, that shall he speak: and he will shew you things to come.

1 John 2:27
27 But the anointing which ye have received of him abideth in you, and ye need not that any man teach you: but as the same anointing teacheth you of all things, and is truth, and is no lie, and even as it hath taught you, ye shall abide in him.

The anointing of the Holy Spirit within us will guide us through the toughest time. As we depend on Him, He will lead us in the way of victory, just as He did the children of Israel.

Psalm 32:8
8 I will instruct thee and teach thee in the way which thou shalt go: I will guide thee with mine eye.

The warmth that the pillar of fire provided speaks of comfort. Jesus called the Holy Spirit "the Comforter" (John 14:26). In the original Greek language in which the New

Testament was written, *comforter* means "counselor, advocate, intercessor; one called alongside to help."

Those words describe the Person I call the "divine therapist"! The Holy Spirit is the only One Who knows the "real you" on the inside! He is the One Who can unlock your true born-again personality and let it shine forth. He does this by illuminating your mind to the truths of the Word of God as you fill your mind with that Word. He reveals areas of your life where you need to yield to Him. He'll heal you and set you free through holy laughter or by leading you into the holy Presence of God in prayer. He'll correct you with the Word of God and lead you to repentance. If you will let Him, He will shape you into a victorious, whole person.

However, I will tell you what the Holy Spirit will *not* do. He will not make you keep reliving the past! He will not bring the "old life" before your mind so you can spend all your time trying to patch it up or figure it out. No! He will bring the "new creation" before your mind and remind you of the person you are now in Christ! He will help you forgive and forget the things of the past and focus on the future.

The Holy Spirit is not only a "force field" of protection and a "divine therapist"—He is also our power source, enabling us to be witnesses unto Jesus!

> **Acts 1:8**
> **8** But ye shall receive power, after that the Holy Ghost is come upon you: and ye shall be witnesses unto me both in Jerusalem, and in all Judaea, and in Samaria, and unto the uttermost part of the earth.

The Greek word translated "witnesses" is *martus*, from which we get our English word *martyr*. A martyr is someone who is so convinced of a truth that he or she will die for it.

The Holy Spirit will put such a conviction of the truth in you that you "die" to your old life—the past—and live in your new life in Christ. You will "know that you know" that you are a new person in Christ—so much so that you will even die physically for this truth rather than deny it.

Just as Jesus *"through the eternal Spirit offered himself without spot to God"* (Heb. 9:14), so the Spirit also helps us offer ourselves to God as living sacrifices, dead to the past and alive with God. And just as Jesus was raised from the dead to a new life, so shall *"the Spirit of him that raised up Jesus from the dead"* quicken us to walk in the new life (Rom. 8:11). We can see then that the Holy Spirit is very much an active agent in our transition from the old life into the new life.

You can know the blessed fellowship of the Holy Spirit in your life. The first prerequisite is that you are a covenant child of God through the blood of Jesus. When the Israelites put their trust in the blood of the slain lamb, they came into covenant with God. That is when the cloud began to manifest to them.

Next, we see in the text that opened this chapter that they *"were all baptized unto Moses in the cloud and in the sea"* (1 Cor. 10:2). It wasn't enough just to have the cloud lead the Israelites out of Egypt. We have already seen that their crossing of the Red Sea was a type of baptism, or burial. But they were also baptized in the cloud, the Holy Spirit.

God wants to "baptize" you, or fill you with the Holy Spirit, primarily so you will be His witness (martyr). That is, so you can put away the "dead man" of your former life and show forth the new life you have in God, which is Christ in you (Col. 1:27).

It would take another book to look thoroughly into this subject. However, you can begin a Holy Spirit-filled life today. First, if you haven't given your life to God, start there! Ask

Jesus to become your Lord. Confess that He is Lord and that He died for you. Surrender your heart to Him. Then ask Jesus Christ to baptize you in the Holy Spirit so you'll have His power in your life to live for Him.

Luke 11:9–13
9 And I say unto you, Ask, and it shall be given you; seek, and ye shall find; knock, and it shall be opened unto you.
10 For every one that asketh receiveth; and he that seeketh findeth; and to him that knocketh it shall be opened.
11 If a son shall ask bread of any of you that is a father, will he give him a stone? or if he ask a fish, will he for a fish give him a serpent?
12 Or if he shall ask an egg, will he offer him a scorpion?
13 If ye then, being evil, know how to give good gifts unto your children: how much more shall your heavenly Father give the Holy Spirit to them that ask him?

This is not a mental experience but a spiritual one. Read the Book of Acts in the New Testament and see what kind of supernatural manifestations accompany those who are filled with God's Spirit! Learn to recognize the Holy Spirit in your life. He will help you forget the land of Egypt, Pharaoh, and the past, and lead you on to the Promised Land!

chapter 7

The Truth Will Make You Free!

Then said Jesus to those Jews which believed on him, If ye continue in my word, then are ye my disciples indeed; And ye shall know the truth, and the truth shall make you free.

—John 8:31–32

When I hear people quote John 8:32, 99 percent of the time they will say, "the truth shall set you free." But have you ever noticed that *set* and *make* are two different words?

For example, if I want to *set* a bird free from a cage, I open the cage door and I say to the bird, "You're free!" I have just set the bird free.

However, if I want to *make* the bird free, I reach inside the cage, lay hold of the bird, take him out of the cage, and turn him loose. It takes an effort on my part.

God didn't just set us free. He opened the door and *made* us free. It took an effort on His part. He took us from the old world and thrust us into the new world. He has *made* us free. He doesn't want us to go back into the cage.

Maybe you are asking as the Jews did in John 8:33, "What do you mean, 'You shall be made free?' Free from what?" Jesus explained that in the next few verses:

John 8:34–36
34 Jesus answered them, Verily, verily, I say unto you, Whosoever committeth sin is the servant of sin.
35 And the servant abideth not in the house for ever: but the Son abideth ever.
36 If the Son therefore shall make you free, ye shall be free indeed.

We could also say it like this: "The Son will make you free from the old life of sin and all its bondages." Or to put it more plainly: Jesus will make you free from your past.

How did Jesus say we would be made free? He said first, "If you continue in My Word" (John 8:22). If you do that, then "*. . . ye shall know the truth, and the truth shall make you free.*"

What does it mean to "continue" in Jesus' Word? James the Apostle said it this way:

James 1:23–25
23 For if any be a hearer of the word, and not a doer, he is like unto a man beholding his natural face in a glass:
24 For he beholdeth himself, and goeth his way, and straightway forgetteth what manner of man he was.
25 But whoso looketh into the perfect law of liberty, and continueth therein, he being not a forgetful hearer, but a doer of the work, this man shall be blessed in his deed.

James called the Word of God the perfect law of liberty. He said we look into it as we would look into a mirror, and we continue to walk in what we see. What do we see when we look into the mirror of God's Word?

Well, when we look at ourselves in a mirror, we see an image of what we look like. When we look into the mirror of God's perfect law of liberty, we see an image of ourselves *as God sees us. We see who we really are in Christ!*

In James 1:25, James mentions the "law of liberty." In Romans 8:2 Paul uses another term: "the law of the Spirit of life." Paul says the way to overcome the law of sin and death is by the law of the Spirit. I am a licensed pilot, so I like to explain it this way: On this planet we are all bound by the law of gravity. The only way to get free from the law of gravity is by using a higher law—one that supersedes the law of gravity. In aviation we call it "the law of lift."

That is, as I sit at the controls of an airplane, ready for takeoff, and I push the throttle in and start rolling down the runway, picking up speed, soon the law of lift takes over. As it does, I find myself being freed from the effects of the law of gravity and soaring into the sky.

As long as I continue operating in the higher law of lift, I will be free from gravity's hold. If I pull back the throttle and lose lift, gravity takes over and down I start to go!

Galatians 5:16 says, *"Walk in the Spirit, and ye shall not fulfill the lust of the flesh."* By walking in "the law of the Spirit," we are free from the hold of the law of sin.

In James 1:22–25, James says to continue in "the law of liberty" by hearing the Word of God and continuing to remember what you see reflected there of who you are in Christ! In other words, see yourself as you are described in the Word of God—what God says you are—and act like that!

Don't act like what you *feel* like, whether physically, emotionally, mentally, or any other way. Act like what God says you are!

When I was a new believer, I still had a consciousness of sin because of my past. I had a tendency to see myself in a negative light. For instance, when I was reading through the

Book of Proverbs, I noticed a lot of verses that had both a negative and a positive implication. A typical verse would have something to say about both the righteous and the wicked, or the wise man and the fool. As I read those verses, I would have a tendency in my mind to gravitate toward the negative, because I didn't see myself as a righteous or wise man.

But praise God! One day He opened my eyes to my position in Christ, and I began to see myself from God's point of view. I saw that He had made me righteous before Him.

Then I began to read those verses and put myself in the position of the wise or righteous man, and I claimed the promise associated with that position.

For example, when I read Proverbs 15:29, *"The Lord is far from the wicked: but he heareth the prayer of the righteous,"* I saw myself as the righteous man whose prayer God hears.

So how do you continue in God's Word—the perfect law of liberty? You see what God says about you in His Word and you accept that as who you really are. That is your true identity.

Here are some examples of God's image of you as reflected in the mirror of His Word:

- You are the righteousness of God (2 Cor. 5:21).
- You are accepted in the beloved (Eph. 1:6).
- You are holy, chosen, royal (1 Peter 2:9).
- You are light (Eph. 5:8).
- You are a king and priest (Rev. 1:6).
- You are God's child (1 John 3:1–2).
- You are anointed (2 Cor. 1:21).

- You are called, justified, and glorified (Rom. 8:30).
- You are dead to sin (1 Peter 2:24).
- You are healed (1 Peter 2:24).
- You are alive unto God (Rom. 6:11).
- You are crucified with Christ (Gal. 2:20).
- You are dead, buried, and risen with Christ (Col. 2:12–13; 3:1).

Taking these few scriptures and making them your confession will have a profound effect on your life. The word *confess* means "to say the same thing; to agree with." When you confess what God's Word says about you as the truth and you start to act as if it is true, you are continuing in the "law of liberty." You are not being a forgetful hearer but a doer of the Word (James 1:22–25).

These are just a few of the many things God has to say about who and what you are in Christ. As you continue in this Word—confessing that the person it describes is who you really are, and acting as if that is who you are—Jesus said you would come to know the truth, and this truth would make you free from sin!

Begin to see yourself as a new creature in Him, dead to the past. As you do, you will be made free from the sin consciousness that keeps you in bondage to the past.

Romans 6:11 says, *"Likewise reckon ye also yourselves to be dead indeed unto sin, but alive unto God through Jesus Christ our Lord."* "To reckon" means "to consider." We are to consider ourselves to be dead to sin.

Let's look again at our opening verses for this chapter: "*Then said Jesus to those Jews which believed on him, If ye continue in my word, then are ye my disciples indeed; And ye shall know the truth, and the truth shall make you free*" (John 8:31–32). Notice what Jesus did *not* say in verse 32: "If you continue to talk about the past, try to relive it in your mind, and live in constant remorse over your past failures, then you'll be made free." No! Jesus did not say that! Yet many believers are being sold that lie from the devil.

I've been walking with God since 1971. I was saved during the "Jesus Movement" in California. Then I was involved in the "Charismatic Movement" and the "Faith Movement."

I've seen from the inside the extreme "deliverance" movement of the '70s and the "inner healing" movement of the '80s. Now the same types of things (under different names) are going around again. I call them substitutes for a revival from Heaven. These philosophies all have the same spirit about them. The people who follow them can be described in this scripture:

2 Timothy 3:7
7 Ever learning, and never able to come to the knowledge of the truth.

You see, under these "substitute" teachings, you never quite arrive. There is always another demon to cast out or another area of the past to dig up before you're made whole. Some people who follow these teachings have become so preoccupied with trying to patch themselves up that they don't fulfill the call of God on their lives!

Among the people I know of who have followed these extreme teachings, I never did observe one who had "arrived." Their lives were a never-ending cycle of focusing on one area after another that needed help.

Jesus said you can tell a tree by its fruit (Matt. 12:33). The fruit I observed from these teachings was a group of believers who were so introverted and concerned with their own therapy that they never became effective in being used of God to reach the lost.

Jesus said when you know the truth, you will be made free. What is the truth? The whole purpose of this book is to show you the truth about what God has done for you and in you through your salvation in Jesus Christ. If you are in Christ, you are exactly what the Bible says you are: a new creation. The old has passed away! As you continue in God's Word, the knowledge of that truth will make you free.

When you realize that, right now—even with all your imperfections and hang-ups—you are a new person, and that God can use you *now*, it will free you up on the inside! Glory to God!

Jesus and the Fishermen

Let me give you another illustration from the Word of God to show you what I'm talking about. In the story of Jesus and the fishermen in Luke chapter 5, we find that the Apostle Peter was no doubt frustrated and angry after fishing all night without results. Jesus came along and asked Peter to let Him teach the people along the shoreline from his boat. When He finished speaking, Jesus said to Peter, "Launch out into the deep for a catch" (v. 4). Peter started to argue but then reluctantly agreed, saying, *" . . . nevertheless at thy word I will let down the net"* (v. 5).

You probably know the rest of the story. They caught so many fish that the boat began to sink and the net began to break. They had to call the other boats over to help them bring in the load of fish (vv. 6–7).

What did Peter do next? He fell at Jesus' feet and said, ". . . Depart from me; for I am a sinful man, O Lord" (v. 8). In other words, Peter said, "Lord, I see you are holy, so leave me alone so I can work some more on my life and make it fit for You; I am not a whole, perfect human yet."

And what was Jesus' response? *". . . Fear not; from henceforth thou shalt catch men"* (v. 10). In other words, Jesus didn't want to hear Peter's excuses. He wanted him to get busy and work for God!

The prophet Isaiah had a similar experience, described in Isaiah chapter 6. He saw the Glory of God and said, *"Woe is me! for I am undone; because I am a man of unclean lips . . ."* (v. 5).

God seemed to pay no attention to Isaiah's fearful words. Instead, an angel took a purifying coal from off the altar and touched his lips. Then God asked, *"Whom shall I send, and who will go for us?"* (v. 8).

With both Peter and Isaiah, God was not so much interested in their self-abasement at their awareness of their own sin in His Presence as He was in their willingness and availability to work for Him.

This is what the Lord is saying to you today. You can spend the rest of your life trying to fix up the "old man." Or you can rise up like Peter, walk as the new creation God made you to be, and fulfill your destiny in God!

chapter 8

The Bread and Wine of Deliverance

For I have received of the Lord that which also I delivered unto you, That the Lord Jesus the same night in which he was betrayed took bread: And when he had given thanks, he brake it, and said, Take, eat: this is my body, which is broken for you: this do in remembrance of me. After the same manner also he took the cup, when he had supped, saying, This cup is the new testament in my blood: this do ye, as oft as ye drink it, in remembrance of me. For as often as ye eat this bread, and drink this cup, ye do shew the Lord's death till he come.

—1 Corinthians 11:23–26

The two main sacraments of the Church are Baptism and Communion. We saw earlier that baptism shows forth the wonderful truth we are discussing in this book: we have been delivered from the past.

Water baptism gives us a picture of our deliverance from our past life of sin. Our baptism is like the experience of the children of Israel passing through the Red Sea to leave behind Egypt's bondage, or like Noah entering the Ark through which he was delivered from the former world.

Can we also see this truth portrayed in the sacrament of Communion? Absolutely!

First, what is Communion? To understand this we must go back to the very first Passover meal. You see, when Jesus ate what we call the Last Supper with His disciples, He was in fact celebrating the Passover with them. Among other things, the Passover meal consisted of lamb, unleavened bread, and wine. The night of the first Passover meal, just before the Israelites' deliverance from Egypt, the blood of a lamb was applied to the doorposts of their houses, and they roasted and ate the lamb's flesh.

So the new life of the children of Israel as people freed from slavery started with the blood of a lamb and continued with a meal, then their deliverance from Egypt, and finally their crossing of the Red Sea. You might say *the blood brought them out, and the flood kept them out*!

Now we walk down the corridors of history to the moment of the last Passover meal Jesus celebrated on earth. It was the unleavened Passover bread that He took when He said, *"Take, eat: this is my body which is broken for you"* (1 Cor. 11:24). Jesus, the Lamb of God, gave His body, "broken" for us!

The prophet Isaiah said, *". . . the Lord hath laid on him* [Jesus] *the iniquity of us all"* (Isa. 53:6).

Saint Paul said in Second Corinthians 5:21, *"For he hath made him* [Jesus] *to be sin for us, who knew no sin; that we might be made the righteousness of God in him."* And again, in Galatians 3:13, Paul said, *"Christ hath redeemed us from the curse of the law, being made a curse for us: for it is written, Cursed is every one that hangeth on a tree."*

Jesus took our place under the judgment of God. He became the object of God's wrath, and in doing that Jesus *"delivered us from the wrath to come"* (1 Thess. 1:10). Now,

"God hath not appointed us to wrath, but to obtain salvation by our Lord Jesus Christ" (1 Thess. 5:9).

We saw earlier that Noah's ark represented Jesus Christ's body under the judgment of God for us. Not only was His body the sacrifice for our sins, but we were *in Him* when He died. Our sinful nature was put to death when His body died on that cross.

You could say that Jesus' broken body received the "flood" of God's judgment, and we were safe in Him. Romans 6:4 says, *"Therefore we are buried with him by baptism into death . . . ."*

We also saw in an earlier chapter that the Red Sea crossing was a type of baptism into Him. In Philippians 3:10 Paul refers to this great truth as "the fellowship of his sufferings"—that is, knowing the full meaning and benefit of our partaking of Jesus' death, burial, and resurrection.

Because Jesus gave His body as a sacrifice, broken for us, we have been delivered from our sinful past.

1 Peter 2:24
24 Who his own self bare our sins in his own body on the tree, that we, being dead to sins, should live unto righteousness . . . .

So the bread of Communion reminds us of Jesus' body, which suffered the consequences of our sin so we could live a new life with Him, separated from our past, when He was raised from the dead. What about the Communion cup that we drink? The cup that Jesus held up during that "Last Supper" was the Passover cup. He said, *"This cup is the new testament in my blood . . ."* (1 Cor. 11:25).

We saw in an earlier chapter in this book how the blood of the lamb applied to the doorposts of the Israelites' houses protected them from the destroyer and opened up the way of escape to them. During the Last Supper—which was the first Communion—Jesus showed a direct link between His blood and the blood of the sacrificial Passover lamb.

It is Jesus' blood that delivered us from this world—from sin, hell, and, ultimately, death. And it is Jesus' blood that continues to work in us that deliverance that He wrought on our behalf for all time!

Hebrews 13:20–21
20 Now the God of peace, that brought again from the dead our Lord Jesus, that great shepherd of the sheep, THROUGH THE BLOOD OF THE EVERLASTING COVENANT,
21 Make you perfect in every good work to do his will, working in you that which is wellpleasing in his sight, through Jesus Christ; to whom be glory for ever and ever. Amen.

You have probably heard the phrase, "draw a line in the sand." It means to draw a dividing line, and crossing over that line is significant in some way. Well, Jesus drew a line with His blood. Everyone who is on the "faith" side of that line belongs to Him and is separated from the devil's authority. When we accepted Jesus as our Savior, the devil lost all legal power and authority over us through Jesus' blood!

Romans 5:9
9 Much more then, being now justified by his blood, we shall be saved from wrath through him.

How are we justified by faith in Jesus' blood? Consider for a moment the Old Testament tabernacle and temple. They contained three sections: the outer court, the inner court, and the Holy of Holies. Everyone could enter the outer court, but only the priests could enter the inner court. And only one man—the high priest—could enter the Holy of Holies. He could only do that once a year, when he made sacrifice for the sins of the nation on the Day of Atonement.

The Holy of Holies contained the Ark of the Covenant—the gold-covered wooden box that held the stone tablets bearing the Ten Commandments; the vessel full of manna; and Aaron's rod that had budded and produced almonds. The lid of the Ark, called the "Mercy Seat," was decorated with the figures of two angelic beings, or cherubim, made of gold.

The high priest would enter the Holy of Holies with the blood of a sacrificed animal and put the blood on this Mercy Seat to obtain forgiveness for the sins of the nation. Then the cloud of God's glory—the Holy Spirit—would descend on that Mercy Seat between the cherubim and God would speak to the High Priest. The Lord could bless the nation for the next year because their sins were forgiven.

Now consider the following verses:

> **Romans 3:25–26**
> **25** Whom God hath set forth to be a propitiation through faith in his blood, to declare his righteousness for the remission of sins that are past, through the forbearance of God;
> **26** To declare, I say, at this time his righteousness: that he might be just, and the justifier of him which believeth in Jesus.

These verses tell us God made Jesus the "propitiation" for our sins through faith in His blood. The New Testament was written in Greek, and the Greek word translated "propitiation" can also be translated "Mercy Seat."

In other words, when we put our faith in Jesus' blood, Jesus becomes our Mercy Seat! That means God won't look on our sin, and the Holy Spirit can dwell within us! Glory to God!

Let's take it further. The New Testament says we are now the temple of the Holy Spirit.

1 Corinthians 6:19
19 What? know ye not that your body is the temple of the Holy Ghost which is in you, which ye have of God, and ye are not your own?

Just like the Old Testament temple, we have three parts to us: spirit, soul, and body.

1 Thessalonians 5:23
23 And the very God of peace sanctify you wholly; and I pray God your whole spirit and soul and body be preserved blameless unto the coming of our Lord Jesus Christ.

As with the outer court of the Old Testament temple, our body is connected to this world. Our soul is like the inner court—spiritual activity takes place there, but God doesn't dwell in our mind, will, or emotions. He lives in our born-again spirit, because He is a Spirit, as we see in John chapter 4.

John 4:24
24 God is a Spirit: and they that worship him must worship him in spirit and in truth.

Also, as with the Old Testament example of the Holy of Holies, the born-again human spirit is where God's Law is housed. We see that in Jeremiah chapter 31.

Jeremiah 31:33
33 But this shall be the covenant that I will make with the house of Israel; After those days, saith the Lord, I will put my law in

their inward parts, and write it in their hearts; and will be their God, and they shall be my people.

Under the Old Covenant, the Holy of Holies also was where the manna was kept. We see the New Covenant parallel in John chapter 6.

John 6:51
51 I am the living bread which came down from heaven: if any man eat of this bread, he shall live for ever: and the bread that I will give is my flesh, which I will give for the life of the world.

Also, Aaron's rod was in the Old Testament Holy of Holies. That rod represented authority. According to the Scriptures, Aaron's rod budded and produced almonds as a sign of God's authority on him (see Num. 17:1–8). Aaron's rod parallels the New Testament authority we have in Christ.

All of this has come to us because Jesus has become the Mercy Seat for us through our faith in His blood! We see this more clearly in the following verse from Romans:

Romans 3:25 (*Amplified*)
25 Whom God put forward [before the eyes of all] as a mercy seat and propitiation by His blood [the cleansing and life-giving sacrifice of atonement and reconciliation, to be received] through faith. This was to show God's righteousness, because in His divine forbearance He had passed over and ignored former sins without punishment.

I'd like us to consider one final thought along these lines. If each time we take Communion we show forth the Lord's death, we should take a look at that moment on the cross when He died.

We know from John's account of the Crucifixion that after Jesus had died, a Roman soldier, in order to make sure He was indeed dead, thrust a spear into Jesus' side.

John 19:34
34 But one of the soldiers with a spear pierced his side, and forthwith came there out blood and water.

The Apostle John later said the following in one of his letters:

1 John 5:6–8
6 This is he that came by water and blood, even Jesus Christ; not by water only, but by water and blood. And it is the Spirit that beareth witness, because the Spirit is truth.
7 For there are three that bear record in heaven, the Father, the Word, and the Holy Ghost: and these three are one.
8 And there are three that bear witness in earth, the spirit, and the water, and the blood: and these three agree in one.

On that cross blood and water flowed out—"the blood and the flood" that separated us from the world. And notice also that the "cloud" of God's Presence—the Holy Spirit—also bears witness. Glory to God!

In our opening scripture for this chapter Paul said, "*For as often as ye eat this bread, and drink this cup, ye do shew the Lord's death till he come*" (1 Cor. 11:26). Every time you partake of Communion, you remember Jesus' death. And every time you remember His death, you should remember yours also! You were crucified with Him. The bread and wine of Communion remind us of our deliverance from sin, Satan, and the world.

Never look at Communion the same way again. It's not just a ritual. It's an experience—a confession of faith and an act of faith in the finished work of Calvary.

Drinking of the Communion cup and eating the Communion bread can help you realize what a great work of deliverance has been done in you! Communion can remind you that your past life is forever cut off and you can never go back.

The sacrament of Communion gives us a picture of our deliverance from the past, the world, and the authority of the devil, just as the sacrament of Baptism does.

chapter 9

Seated in Heavenly Places

But God, who is rich in mercy, for his great love wherewith he loved us, Even when we were dead in sins, hath quickened us together with Christ, (by grace ye are saved;) And hath raised us up together, and made us sit together in heavenly places in Christ Jesus.

—Ephesians 2:4–6

Not only were we crucified with Christ (Gal. 2:20) . . .

Not only did we die with Him (Rom. 6:8) . . .

Not only were we buried with Him in baptism (Rom. 6:4) . . .

Not only have we been born again through His resurrection (Rom. 6:4, 11) . . .

. . . but when He ascended on High we were raised up to sit with Him in heavenly places! This is also part of Christ's redemptive work!

Jesus' ascension into Heaven is described in Acts chapter 1:

Acts 1:9–11

9 And when he had spoken these things, while they beheld, he was taken up; and a cloud received him out of their sight.

10 And while they looked stedfastly toward heaven as he went up, behold, two men stood by them in white apparel;

> **11** Which also said, Ye men of Galilee, why stand ye gazing up into heaven? this same Jesus, which is taken up from you into heaven, shall so come in like manner as ye have seen him go into heaven.

We were in Him when He was crucified, when He died, when He was buried, and when He was resurrected from the grave. And we were also in Him when He ascended. Each of these phases was part of the whole redemptive process.

1. When Jesus was crucified, He became sin for us (2 Cor. 5:21), and He became a curse (Gal. 3:13). He became our sin offering.

2. When Jesus died, He paid the price for our sin. The price was death and separation from the Father. He became our scapegoat.

3. When Jesus was buried, He closed the door to the past. (Death is "finality.") It was final! The sin He bore had no more power!

4. When Jesus was resurrected, it meant absolute victory over death, devils, sickness, and sin, and all that is associated with sin. It meant a new beginning. His resurrection made righteousness available to us (Rom. 4:25).

5. When Jesus ascended into Heaven to sit down at the right hand of the Father, it signified His authority and rule. And we are seated with Him in the heavenlies (Eph. 2:6).

> **Romans 4:22–25**
> **22** And therefore it was imputed to him for righteousness.
> **23** NOW IT WAS NOT WRITTEN FOR HIS SAKE ALONE, that it was imputed to him;
> **24** BUT TO US ALSO, to whom it shall be imputed, if we believe on him that raised up Jesus our Lord from the dead;

25 Who was delivered for our offences, and was raised again
for our justification.

Ephesians 1:20–22
20 Which he wrought in Christ, when he raised him from the
dead, and set him at his own right hand in the heavenly places,
21 Far above all principality, and power, and might, and
dominion, and every name that is named, not only in this
world, but also in that which is to come:
22 And hath put all things under his feet, and gave him to be
the head over all things to the church.

All of mankind was represented in Christ when He accomplished all of these things (2 Cor. 5:19). So where does that leave us now as believers? It leaves us where Jesus Christ is now—seated in the heavenlies! In other words, it leaves us in a place of spiritual authority, seated with Him. The following verses in Hebrews chapter 12 describe where we are because we have accepted Jesus as our Savior:

Hebrews 12:22–24
22 But ye are come unto mount Sion, and unto the city of the
living God, the heavenly Jerusalem, and to an innumerable
company of angels,
23 To the general assembly and church of the firstborn, which
are written in heaven, and to God the Judge of all, and to the
spirits of just men made perfect,
24 And to Jesus the mediator of the new covenant, and to the
blood of sprinkling, that speaketh better things than that
of Abel.

I heard a preacher say it like this: "In the same way He is as much *here* (with us) as He is *there* (in Heaven), so we are as much *there* (in the heavenlies) as we are *here* (on the earth)." And our position in Christ is a place of authority, as the following verse points out:

Romans 5:17
17 much more they which receive abundance of grace and of the gift of righteousness shall reign in life by one, Jesus Christ.

As this verse says, thanks to Jesus and our place in Him, we can now reign in life. We can walk daily in victory, not defeat!

Does this sound strange to you? Look carefully at the following verses:

Revelation 1:5–6
5 And from Jesus Christ, who is the faithful witness, and the first begotten of the dead, and THE PRINCE OF THE KINGS OF THE EARTH. Unto him that loved us, and washed us from our sins in his own blood,
6 And HATH MADE US KINGS AND PRIESTS unto God and his Father; to him be glory and dominion for ever and ever. Amen.

We are the kings that Jesus is Prince and King over (1 Tim. 6:15; Rev. 17:14; 19:16)! We are part of His Kingdom, and He has made us kings to rule under Him.

A king is someone who conquers enemies, claims territory, and establishes rule. When Jesus told His followers to "heal the sick, cast out devils, and preach the Gospel to the poor," He told them to say, "the Kingdom of Heaven is at hand" (Matt. 10:7–8). We know that Jesus wasn't trying to overthrow the Roman government. He was overthrowing the kingdom of darkness!

Every time someone is born again, new territory is taken for the Kingdom of God. Every time someone is delivered from sickness or demons, a prisoner of war has been liberated!

Here is the truth about who we are:

- We are citizens of this new world.
- We are of the heavenlies.
- We are of the spirit world.
- We are of the New Birth.
- We are new creations.
- We are no longer of this world.
- We are pilgrims just passing through this earth.
- We are just visiting here for a while.

When God establishes His Kingdom on the earth, things are going to change. But right now we are not of this world. Right now we are part of another world—the spiritual Kingdom of God. We see that in Colossians chapter 1.

Colossians 1:12–13
12 Giving thanks unto the Father, which hath made us meet to
be partakers of the inheritance of the saints in light:
13 Who hath delivered us from the power of darkness, AND
HATH TRANSLATED US INTO THE KINGDOM OF HIS DEAR SON.

Just as the eight souls in Noah's ark were translated into a new world, and just as the Children of Israel were translated into a new land, so God has translated us into the Kingdom of His dear Son.

We were once under the devil's authority and his dominion, but not anymore.

Ephesians 2:2
2 Wherein IN TIME PAST ye walked according to the course of this world, according to the prince of the power of the air, the spirit that now worketh in the children of disobedience.

We were slaves in Egypt, so to speak. But praise God, we have come out of Egypt and have been translated into a new life! The old man is dead and passed away, and a new creation has come!

As believers in Jesus Christ, we are living in two worlds at the same time. Through our physical bodies we are connected to this world. Through our spirit we are connected to Heaven.

Spiritually, we are alive unto God—born of His Spirit and connected to Him through our spirit.

1 Corinthians 6:17

17 But he that is joined unto the Lord is one spirit.

Our old nature (the Bible calls it "the old man") was crucified with Christ. We are dead to sin. The new man is our recreated human spirit. This is our new nature, our true self.

Colossians 3:9–10

9 Lie not one to another, seeing that ye have put off the old man with his deeds;

10 AND HAVE PUT ON THE NEW MAN, which is renewed in knowledge after the image of him that created him. . . .

Ephesians 4:24

24 AND THAT YE PUT ON THE NEW MAN, which after God is created in righteousness and true holiness.

Our bodies are mortal. They're still connected to this world. We are instructed to consider them as dead to sin (Rom. 6:11). We are crucified with Christ.

Galatians 2:20
20 I am crucified with Christ: nevertheless I live; yet not I, but Christ liveth in me: and the life which I now live in the flesh I live by the faith of the Son of God, who loved me, and gave himself for me.

The redemption that Jesus purchased for us with His blood will be completed in us when our bodies are changed to be like His—immortal and incorruptible.

In the meantime, we are to control our bodies through the Holy Spirit Who lives in us. Our bodies are now His temple. He can dwell in us because of the blood of Jesus—our Mercy Seat.

We are not to be dominated by our bodies. We are to master our bodies with the help of the Spirit of God in us.

Romans 8:13
13 For if ye live after the flesh, ye shall die: but if ye through the Spirit do mortify the deeds of the body, ye shall live.

We are to learn to let the Holy Spirit lead us, and in so doing we will not allow the flesh to rule us. We are to let our "new man" on the inside (who is seated with Jesus Christ in the heavenlies) rule over our outer man—our flesh—that is connected to this earthly realm.

chapter 10

A New Power Source

Let's recall a couple of key points we've seen so far in this book. When we accepted Jesus as our Savior, we trusted that the blood He shed on the Cross at Calvary paid the price for our sins. And our baptism in water painted a picture of our identification with Christ. When He died, we died. When He was buried, we were buried. When He rose again to new life, we rose with Him.

When the Children of Israel were in bondage in Egypt, the blood of a lamb without blemish applied to the doorposts of their houses was a sign of their deliverance from slavery. And their passage through the Red Sea separated them once and for all from their past.

We've come through the blood and through the flood, just as they did. We are new creatures in Christ and we can never again go back to who we once were.

You don't need to fear Pharaoh and his army—or, in other words, the devil—chasing you. The lies and habits of your past are just that—they're of the past. They're ghosts. The old you—your "old man"—is dead. That's nothing but a dead man chasing you! You don't have to return to old bondages.

A "double death" took place at Calvary. We died to the world, and the world died to us.

Galatians 6:14
14 But God forbid that I should glory, save in the cross of our Lord Jesus Christ, by whom the world is crucified unto me, and I unto the world.

The Bible says we are to look at ourselves as dead to the past and to the world (Rom. 6:11). It also says that because we are risen with Christ, we are to seek those things which are above (Col. 3:1). This is the Bible way to victory! The way we deal with past hurts and sins is to realize that the past is dead!

Now, you may be thinking, "I know my past before I became a Christian is dead, but I've really failed God miserably since the time I was saved."

You must consider your old life dead. Sinful actions don't come from your born-again spirit. They come from your acting under the influence of your "old man."

No, a Christian does not sin by acting in accordance with his new nature. He sins by letting his old life (which is dead) influence his thoughts and actions.

The way to stop this is not to try to "fix" the old but to pursue the new! Consider your old life dead and chase after the new life that is yours in Christ!

You must deal with sin in your life the same way you deal with sickness—by faith. Many believers are learning that in order to deal with sickness, they must stand on the "past tense" of God's Word. In other words, they must realize that Jesus Christ took their sickness upon Himself on the Cross.

He totally paid the price for their healing, and therefore in Him they were healed. Look at the following words in First Peter chapter 2:

1 Peter 2:24
24... by whose stripes ye WERE healed.

When you appropriate that promise in your life as an accomplished fact, healing power works in your body.

The Bible also says to "reckon" (or consider) yourself to be dead to sin (Rom. 6:11). If you were facing symptoms of sickness in your body, you would stand in faith against those symptoms and say, "I know that I am healed by Jesus' stripes" (Isa. 53:5). In the same way, you must look at your sin and say, "God, I confess my sin to You. I acknowledge that I've missed it. I thank You for the blood of Jesus that cleanses me from all unrighteousness (1 John 1:7), and I thank You that I am born of Your Spirit (John 3:5). The old me is dead and gone, and I don't desire to do those things anymore that the old me did. I am a new creation in You."

The more you consider yourself to be dead to sin and alive to God, the more you will act like it!

You see, a conscience that is guilt-ridden because of past sins that have been confessed and forgiven is like a magnet that keeps pulling you back into failure. Jesus knew that. (I wish some religious preachers would figure it out!) Jesus said to the woman caught in adultery, *". . . Neither do I condemn thee: go, and sin no more"* (John 8:11).

When people know they are really forgiven of their sin, that sin is no longer attractive to them. Only Jesus is attractive to them!

Consider the story in Luke chapter 7 of the woman who came to Jesus and anointed His feet with her tears (Luke 7:36–50). The religious Pharisee judged her in his heart because she was a "sinner." Jesus told him a story of two men who owed debts to a certain person. One owed a small amount, and the other a huge debt. The creditor canceled the debts of both men. Jesus asked, "Which of them will love the creditor the most?"

The Pharisee answered Jesus correctly: the one who was forgiven the most. Jesus then proceeded to tell him that the woman knew that her many sins were forgiven. Therefore, she was showing her love and appreciation to the Lord. The secret to motivating people to love God and hate sin is to open their eyes to the forgiveness that already belongs to them in Jesus Christ!

I wish some people could get that through their "religious" minds! Instead of condemning and criticizing people, they should be showing them what a wonderful salvation Jesus has provided for them. Anyone can come to Him, put the past behind them, become a new creation in Jesus, and enter into new life in Him!

My point is this: We must not major on failure—either our own or others'—but on what God has provided for us in Jesus Christ! We must focus on the new creation that we are in Christ.

There is a profound truth in the Book of Romans that most of the Church has never understood. We see it in chapter 8:

Romans 8:9–11
9 But ye are not in the flesh, but in the Spirit, if so be that the Spirit of God dwell in you. Now if any man have not the Spirit of Christ, he is none of his.
10 And if Christ be in you, the body is dead because of sin; but the Spirit is life because of righteousness.

11 But if the Spirit of him that raised up Jesus from the dead dwell in you, he that raised up Christ from the dead shall also quicken your mortal bodies by his Spirit that dwelleth in you.

Now I want you to see the same verses in the *New International Version.*

Romans 8:9–11 (*NIV*)
9 You, however, are controlled not by the sinful nature but by the Spirit, if the Spirit of God lives in you. And if anyone does not have the Spirit of Christ, he does not belong to Christ.
10 But if Christ is in you, your body is dead because of sin, yet your spirit is alive because of righteousness.
11 And if the Spirit of him who raised Jesus from the dead is living in you, he who raised Christ from the dead will also give life to your mortal bodies through his Spirit, who lives in you.

As far as God is concerned, if you are in Christ and He is in you, your body of sin is dead, but your spirit is alive. And your body is now kept alive by the Spirit of God within you. Various translations of verse 10 show that your body is dead but your spirit is alive. And according to verse 11, the resurrection power of the Holy Spirit now "quickens" or "gives life to" your physical body.

In Romans 8:12 the Apostle Paul said that because the Spirit makes us alive, we are no longer debtors to the flesh. We don't owe our allegiance to the sinful flesh anymore!

Paul said the same thing another way in his letter to the Church in Galatia:

Galatians 2:20
20 I am crucified with Christ: nevertheless I live; yet not I, but Christ liveth in me: AND THE LIFE WHICH I NOW LIVE IN THE FLESH I LIVE BY THE FAITH OF THE SON OF GOD, who loved me, and gave himself for me.

It is as though you have changed the "power source" of your life.

God gave me an illustration that helped me understand this. I fly quite frequently, both on commercial airlines and piloting my own airplane. On one commercial flight, after we had boarded and were sitting at the gate waiting to depart, I noticed after the crew started the engines that the lights went off in the cabin for a few seconds. Then they abruptly came on again.

I knew what was happening. Before the engines were started, the airliner received electric power from a cable attached to the airport terminal. After the engines were running, the ground crew disconnected the electrical power cable from the terminal and the cockpit crew switched to onboard power. We had changed the source of the power for the lights.

No longer did the aircraft have to be "plugged in" to the earth for its power. Now it was generating its own power from within. We weren't bound to the earth anymore. We could fly off into the sky and have all the power we needed coming from within the plane.

That is what Paul was saying in Galatians 2:20. Once we have accepted Jesus as our Savior, our old life is dead—crucified with Him! The life we now live in our earthly bodies is energized by a new power source!

When you become a believer in Jesus, your very life is sustained by "the faith of the Son of God." What is that faith? It is the same faith Jesus was walking in when He said about His life, *"No man taketh it from me, but I lay it down of myself. I have power to lay it down, and I have power to take it again . . ."* (John 10:18).

That's resurrection power! That power is the Spirit of God Who raised Jesus from the dead—the same Spirit Who dwells in every believer!

There is an old song I used to sing in certain Pentecostal groups. It went something like this:

It's the Holy Ghost and fire, and it's keeping me alive,
Keeping me alive, keeping me alive.
It's the Holy Ghost and fire, and it's keeping me alive.
Jesus is keeping me alive!

I wonder if the old-time Pentecostals knew the significance of what they were singing. Too few believers have ever lived in the full revelation of this truth. Some, like Smith Wigglesworth and John G. Lake, have lived in it and have shaken their generation with the power of God.

The only death a believer will experience is the one he encounters when he first comes to Christ, dies to his old life, and is born again. After that, when our physical body wears out or expires, we are simply laying it aside while we go to be with the Lord, waiting for that Resurrection Day when the last trumpet will sound, the dead will be raised, and He will reconstruct that body into an immortal one like His (1 Cor. 15:51–52)! We see this in the following verse:

Philippians 3:21
21 Who shall change our vile body, that it may be fashioned like unto his glorious body.

One day our physical bodies will undergo a change and be transformed into immortal, glorified bodies like Jesus Christ's own body. Until then, we are to consider our bodies dead, crucified with Him. And we are to consider that we are now sustained in this life by the Spirit of God within us.

Romans 8:10–11 (*NIV*)
10 But if Christ is in you, your body is dead because of sin, yet
your spirit is alive because of righteousness.
11 And if the Spirit of him who raised Jesus from the dead is
living in you, he who raised Christ from the dead will also give
life to your mortal bodies through his Spirit, who lives in you.

We don't draw our life from this world—we draw it from the same Spirit that raised Jesus Christ from the dead.

When you were born again, or "saved," your spirit was created brand-new in an instant. Now, as you live each day as a follower of Jesus Christ, your soul—which includes your emotions, mind, and will—is being renewed every day. And your physical body awaits the full effect of redemption, which takes place at the resurrection of the bodies of Christians who have died (1 Cor. 15:51–52).

Romans 8:23
23 And not only they, but ourselves also, which have the first-fruits of the Spirit, even we ourselves groan within ourselves, waiting for the adoption, to wit, the redemption of our body.

As followers of Jesus Christ, we don't belong to "Egypt" (or this world) any more. We should not let "Pharaoh"—meaning the devil—keep us in slavery to the past.

We are new creatures in Christ Jesus, and we have a new power source within us—the Holy Spirit. He is the same Spirit Who raised Jesus from the dead, and He is making alive our mortal bodies. We need no longer be tied to the ways of the life we lived before we accepted Jesus as our Savior. The person we used to be is dead. Now we are free to pursue our new life in Christ!

Conclusion

What I have endeavored to do in this book is unfold for you the meaning of a simple, yet profound, New Testament truth. It is the key to victory in all areas of life. That truth is this: If you are a Christian, you are dead to your past. You are literally a new person.

As you realize this fact and begin to act as if it is true for you, the bondages of the past will lose their hold on your life. Your conscience will be freed from condemnation and a constant sense of failure, and you will be at liberty to serve the Lord acceptably in faith.

Jesus said the harvest was ripe and ready to be brought in, but the laborers were few (Matt. 9:37). If that was true then—when He spoke to His disciples while He was on the earth—how much more is it true today?

The problem is, many believers who should be helping to bring in the harvest are instead sitting on the edge of the field, caught up in trying to perfect themselves and heal the wounds of their past. They are trying to make themselves "perfect" before thinking about getting involved with the work of God.

The Bible doesn't hide the imperfections of great men and women of God. For example, James tells us something about Elias (Elijah) the prophet:

James 5:17
17 Elias was a man subject to like passions as we are, and he prayed earnestly that it might not rain: and it rained not on the earth by the space of three years and six months.

This verse shows us that even the mighty prophet Elijah had the same struggles with his human flesh that we do. Yet he was still used powerfully by God. I'm not saying that we shouldn't continually try to change and become more like Jesus. I am saying that we don't have to be perfect for God to use us!

Thinking that we must perfect ourselves before God can do anything through us is a trap of the devil designed to keep many able and useful people from fulfilling their destiny. Even if we did "get it together" and feel like we had "arrived," what are we going to do? The devil is not afraid of our efforts in the flesh—our self-effort. If we "get there" in one area, he will just knock us down in some other area. Then we will have to start all over again to patch ourselves up. Self-produced "righteousness" doesn't move God or the devil. It only causes pride in the one doing the so-called "righteous" acts.

Someone has said, "Pride is the only disease that makes everyone sick except the one who has it!" The devil is only frightened of the blood and the Cross of Christ and of those who know how to walk in its finished work. And God blesses those who serve Him by faith in what Jesus has done!

God didn't save you and then tell you to go into the desert for 40 years until you are perfect and "functional" before going to reach the world. No!

It does take preparation time to enter the ministry God has called you to. But when it comes to sharing the Good News with the world, He says, "Go! Freely you have received—freely give it out" (Matt. 10:8). Don't let this glorious salvation that is in you stagnate, tangled up in man-made efforts to perfect that which God calls "dead." You are alive in Him right now!

Jesus said, "The harvest is plentiful but the workers are few. Ask the Lord of the harvest, therefore, to send out workers into his harvest field" (Matt 9:37–38 *NIV*).The problem has always been the lack of people willing and able to help in the work of the Lord. Why? The laborers are sitting around waiting for "someday" when they feel ready to do something for God. They are waiting until they conquer one last demon or mature to one more level.

I tell you, one of the fastest ways to conquer your flesh and move up to a higher level spiritually is to start witnessing to others about Jesus Christ. Get involved in changing other people's lives and you'll soon forget about your own!

"Someday" will never come if you sit around waiting for it. Now is the time to get out of the boat and walk on water with Jesus. Peter was by no means perfect, but he was willing to try! He got out of the boat and walked on water with Jesus!

Most people remember how Peter began to sink because he took his eyes off Jesus. But they must also remember that Peter got back on top of the waves and walked with Jesus on the water back to the boat! I would rather get out of the boat with Jesus and risk failure than be a spectator like the other 11 disciples who stayed in the boat.

Believers have had their eyes on the wrong thing. They have gotten caught up in the process of trying to perfect their own humanity. In so doing, they have forgotten about God's mercy and grace. Consider this verse in Second Corinthians:

> **2 Corinthians 4:7**
> **7** But we have this treasure in earthen vessels, that the excellency of the power may be of God, and not of us.

The treasure that is in us is the very Nature of God—our born-again spirit. When we are born again, God lives in us.

Yet this treasure is in "earthen vessels" or "clay pots." Such containers are fragile and easily broken. Why would God put such a treasure in such a weak vessel? He does it so that it's obvious to all that the power and glory that pours from our lives is not ours—but His!

I pray that through reading this book you have been encouraged to put aside the distractions of guilt, condemnation, and self-effort aimed at pleasing God. I pray that you now will take up the armor of God and help the rest of us bring in the harvest!

When you are tempted to look at your past, remember this: as you turn your head to look back, all you should be able to see is the blood and the flood! Realize that the past is just that—past! You've been delivered through the blood and through the flood!

About the Author

Kirk A. DuBois was delivered from drugs and the occult in 1971 during the "Jesus Movement" in San Diego, California. Days later he was baptized in the Pacific Ocean and began sharing his testimony and preaching the Gospel on the streets and beaches of Southern California and in correctional institutions, rescue missions, home Bible study groups, and churches.

Through the years, Kirk has worked with youth and singles groups in various denominational and nondenominational churches. In response to a vision the Lord gave him to be a part of the last great harvest before Jesus Christ returns, he has ministered in the U.S. and around the world—holding open-air crusades, teaching in Bible schools, and ministering in churches.

Kirk graduated from the Assemblies of God Berean School of the Bible and from RHEMA Bible Training Center in Broken Arrow, Oklahoma, where he is currently an instructor in the school. He and his wife, Pat, have two daughters.